ST/ESA/PAD/SER.E/187

Department of Economic and Social Affairs

Responsive and Accountable Public Governance

2015 WORLD PUBLIC SECTOR REPORT

I0130121

UNITED NATIONS
New York, 2015

DESA Mission Statement

The Department of Economic and Social Affairs of the United Nations Secretariat is a vital interface between global policies in the economic, social and environmental spheres and national action. The Department works in three main interlinked areas: 1) It compiles, generates and analyses a wide range of economic, social and environmental data and information on which States Members of the United Nations draw to review common problems and to take stock of policy options; 2) It facilitates the negotiations of Member States in many intergovernmental bodies on joint courses of action to address ongoing or emerging global challenges; and 3) It advises interested Governments on the ways and means of translating policy frameworks developed in United Nations conferences and summits into programmes at the country level and through technical assistance helps build national capacities. ◆

Note by UNDESA

The designations employed and the presentation of the material in this publication do not imply the expression of any opinion whatsoever on the part of the Secretariat of the United Nations concerning the legal status of any country, territory, city or area or of its authorities or concerning the delimitation of its frontiers or boundaries. The term "country" as used in the text of this publication also refers, as appropriate, to territories and areas. Since there is no established convention for the designation of "developed" and "developing" countries or areas in the United Nations system, this distinction is made for statistical and analytical purposes only and does not necessarily express a judgment about the stage reached by a particular country or region in the development process. Mention of the name of any company, organization, product or website does not imply endorsement on the part of the United Nations. The views expressed in this publication are those of the individual authors (see acknowledgements) and do not imply any expression of opinion on the part of the United Nations.

A United Nations Publication
Publication No.: ST/ESA/PAD/SER.E/187
Copyright © United Nations, 2015

Preface

The 2015 World Public Sector Report (WPSR) analyses responsiveness and accountability as two fundamental principles of governance which are key, cross-cutting enablers of development.

From its inception, the WPSR has addressed a range of contemporary topics in public governance that significantly impact the United Nations Development Agenda, including the Millennium Development Goals (MDGs). All five editions of the WPSR are found at www.unpan.org/DPADM/ProductsServices/WorldPublicSectorReport/ tabid/645/language/en-US/Default.aspx.

As the international community is about to adopt the 2030 Agenda for Sustainable Development, the 2015 WPSR intends to contribute by highlighting critical issues of public governance. It draws on discussions that took place at the 12th and the 13th Session of the United Nations Committee of Experts on Public Administration (CEPA), but particularly the 12th Session on the role of responsive and accountable public governance in achieving the MDGs and the post-2015 development agenda. It also benefits from in-depth contributions from some Committee members. It supplements CEPA's deliberations with initial profiles of selected United Nations Public Administration Country Studies (UNPACS) for 193 Member States. Through UNPACS, the Department of Economic and Social Affairs (DESA) is analysing aspects of public institutional capacity, e-government and citizen engagement.

Since 1948, the United Nations has engaged with its Member States on the importance of building sufficient capacities of their governments for economic and social development.[1] Currently, the Department of Economic and Social Affairs continues to fulfil this support role through its mission of assisting the Member States in fostering efficient, effective, transparent, accountable, and citizen-centred public governance, administration and services through innovation and technology to achieve the internationally agreed development goals.

---

1 See mandate given in resolution 246 (111).

I trust that the 2015 WPSR will serve as a useful reference on how responsive and accountable governance will contribute to sustainable development for attaining the future we want for all.

Juwang Zhu, Director
Division for Public Administration and Development Management
Department of Economic and Social Affairs
United Nations

Acknowledgements

The *2015 World Public Sector Report* (WPSR) was prepared by the Department of Economic and Social Affairs (DESA) of the United Nations, through its Division for Public Administration and Development Management (DPADM).

The WPSR was prepared under the responsibility of Elia Yi Armstrong (former Chief, Development Management Branch) and reviewed by John-Mary Kauzya (Chief, Public Administration Capacity Branch) and Vincenzo Aquaro (Chief, e-Government Branch). Valentina Resta (Senior Governance and Public Administration Officer) coordinated the 2015 WPSR. Garegin Manukyan (Senior Governance and Public Administration Officer), Elida Reci (Governance and Public Administration Officer), Arpine Korekyan (Governance and Public Administration Officer) and Yu Jung Kim (Information Management Officer) assisted with inputs. Michelle Alves de Lima (former Programme Assistant), Nathan Henninger (former Public Information Assistant) and Xiao Wang (Public Information Assistant) provided administrative and document support. Xinxin Cai (Programme Assistant), Audrey Croci, Marco Grosso and Macarena Brechner Vega (Interns) provided research support.

The Division would like to acknowledge the contributions of the members of the United Nations Committee of Experts on Public Administration (CEPA), observers and all other physical and remote participants of CEPA's 12th Session in 2012. The Division also thanks Meredith Edwards (Emeritus Professor, University of Canberra, Australia), Mushtaq Khan (Professor of Economics, University of London, United Kingdom), and Margaret Saner (independent Senior Strategic Adviser on Governance, Leadership, Change and Institution Building, United Kingdom) who provided additional submissions for the WPSR.

The Division would like to also acknowledge the work of two International Consultants: Lois Warner, who summarized the written contributions, and José Urquilla, who reviewed United Nations Public Administration Country Studies (UNPACS) for illustrative findings and presented them in charts.

Executive summary

In August 2015, United Nations Member States reached an agreement on the outcome document that will constitute the 2030 Agenda for Sustainable Development—the development framework beyond the Millennium Development Goals (MDG) target date. At the request of General Assembly, the Secretary-General gave a report that synthesized the full range of inputs as a contribution to the intergovernmental negotiations in the lead up to the Summit on Sustainable Development to be held in New York in September 2015. This synthesis report[2] underscored the importance of strengthening effective, accountable, participatory and inclusive governance among key elements required for implementing a universal agenda for the next 15 years.

The 2015 World Public Sector Report (WPSR), titled *Responsive and Accountable Public Governance*, presents the need for public governance to become more responsive and accountable in order for the State to lead the implementation of a collective vision of sustainable development. Social and technical innovations are providing an opportunity for the social contract between the State and the citizenry to shift towards more collaborative governance.

Sustainable development, as the guiding vision for the new development agenda, calls for integration among different levels, spheres and sectors, creating additional challenges in the processes of governance. By seizing the opportunity and meeting the challenges, all governance stakeholders can craft strategies for accommodating multiple-stakeholder perspectives to produce more responsive and accountable public policies, goods and services for sustainable development.

The Report is presented in four chapters. Chapters 1, 2 and 3 address the following: governance as a priority for development; responsive governance; and accountable governance. Chapter 4 focuses on transformations in public governance that can contribute to sustaining more responsive and accountable governance throughout the next 15 years. Summaries of each chapter are provided below.

Chapter 1 discusses the reciprocal relationship between public governance and development, and analyses their respective challenges. It briefly introduces the evolution of the concept of governance, highlighting the key

---

2 United Nations General Assembly, "The road to dignity by 2030: ending poverty, transforming all lives and protecting the planet", synthesis report of the Secretary-General on the post-2015 sustainable development agenda, A/69/700, 4 December 2014, para. 50, p. 11.

role of public leadership in promoting people-centred development. It presents responsiveness and accountability as the most salient features of governance for effective sustainable development policies and delivery of essential public services.

It points out that, since 1948, the United Nations has continuously worked collaboratively with Member States on strengthening the State and building capacity in their public administrations for economic and social development.

In conclusion, it lists those essential components of responsive and accountable governance for implementing the new sustainable development agenda identified by the United Nations Committee of Experts on Public Administration during its 12th Session: information; innovation; combined global-local approaches and use of socioeconomic indicators; quality, relevance and local proximity of data; local ownership and combination of horizontal and top-down engagement; political competition and inclusion; and knowledge sharing based on good local practices.

Chapter 2 highlights key elements of responsive governance for development, including responding efficiently and effectively to people's needs; meeting increasing public demands and addressing declining public trust among partners and constituents; promoting competent, diverse and ethical public servants; engaging citizens and empowering communities as well as providing for multi-channel service delivery and e-participation. Multisector cooperation and increased public participation are identified as a necessity for responsive action in governance for development. These increase opportunities for identifying, communicating and meeting the most pressing needs.

Challenges encountered in managing partnerships across sectors in the delivery of public goods and services are noted. These stem from differences in values, missions, institutional goals among government, not-for-profit and private sector organizations and the variance in formal versus informal systems that characterize their operations. Addressing these increasingly complex realities requires multidimensional and multidisciplinary approaches in coherent policymaking, while leveraging opportunities available through collaboration with non-State actors.

In conclusion, this chapter emphasizes the need for quality, quantity and prompt delivery of public services. It also emphasizes the importance of equality and equity in their provision and greater access to them, also leveraging ICT in innovative ways. Furthermore, it highlights the importance of competence, professionalism, ethics and diversity within the public service; coherence between formal and informal organizations within societies; as well as multi-sectored partnerships and multiple-stakeholder engagement and participation in decision-making.

Chapter 3 notes that the United Nation Secretary-General has stated, "Effective governance for sustainable development demands that public institutions in all countries and at all levels be inclusive, participatory and accountable to the people".[3] Accountable governance involves providing information or answerability" for decisions and actions as well as dealing with consequences—and, increasingly, the quality of performance—for taking decisions and actions.

Among other results, accountability ensures that public funds are used for the purpose for which they are intended. It helps to ensure that public officials exercise their authority in ways to respect the rule of law and are consistent with public values. By safeguarding appropriate use of revenue raised from taxpayers, it also enhances public trust in governance.

This chapter addresses enhancing accountability by leveraging existing resources and safeguarding new ones; fighting waste, mismanagement and corruption (as outlined in the United Nations Convention against Corruption); transparent and accountable public institutions; shared and social accountability; and e-government and open government data.

This chapter underscores the necessity of reshaping governance through transparent and accountable public institutions, while considering the political contexts of informal institutions for successful governance reforms, and reconciling traditional approaches of accountability with shared responsibility of multiple agencies for shared results.

It concludes with some principles for accountability that can be used in monitoring the implementation activities of the new agenda: clear roles and responsibilities; clear performance expectations; balanced expectations and capacities; credible reporting; and reasonable review and adjustment. It also underscores the importance of e-tools, openness of public data as well as feedback and advice provided by supreme audit institutions and other independent oversight bodies.

Chapter 4 analyses options for transforming governance in anticipation of the requirements of the new development period. The chapter illustrates the importance of responsive and accountable governance for inclusive economic growth, social justice and environmental sustainability, as well as development and governance opportunities for transformative actions.

Opportunities for transforming governance include a more active role by the state in reaching down, out and within to catalyse innovations and localized solutions to development problems; technical innovation that helps

---

3 United Nations General Assembly, "The road to dignity by 2030: ending poverty, transforming all lives and protecting the planet", synthesis report of the Secretary-General on the post-2015 sustainable development agenda, A/69/700, 2014, para. 77, p. 19.

integrate and accelerate delivery on development; and innovative solutions for engaging various stakeholders to effectively gather expertise and proposals on transformative action.

A little over two years after the 2012 Rio+20 conference, an Open Working Group on Sustainable Development Goals (SDGs), composed of representatives of Member States, prepared a proposal for SDGs. Member States agreed that this proposal should be the main component of the new development agenda to be launched in September 2015. The Intergovernmental Committee of Experts on Sustainable Development Financing proposed options for a strategy to mobilize significant resources and the institutional governance mechanisms for their effective use. The United Nations Secretary-General's Independent Expert Advisory Group on a Data Revolution for Sustainable Development (IEAG) highlighted the global challenges of dealing with knowledge gaps, namely, what is known from data and gaps between those who have access to critical information and those who do not as well as proposals for dealing with them. These proposals served as critical inputs to the 2030 Agenda for Sustainable Development to be adopted in a summit at the level of Heads of State and Government in September 2015.

Once the agenda is adopted, the challenge for Member States is to turn it into reality for their citizens. Responsiveness and accountability can move governments from reform to transformation to meet the challenges of implementing the development agenda beyond 2015. Governance, to be both an enabler and an outcome of sustainability, must be innovative, proactive and inclusive.

Abbreviations and acronyms

The following symbols have been used throughout this Report:

, **A comma** is used to indicate thousands.

. **A full stop** is used to indicate decimals.

- **A hyphen** between years, for example 2001-2015, includes the beginning and ending years

The following abbreviations and acronyms have been used in this Report:

APSC	Australian Public Service Commission
CEDAW	Convention on the Elimination of All Forms of Discrimination Against Women
CEPA	United Nations Committee of Experts on Public Administration
CERD	International Convention on Elimination of All Forms of Racial Discrimination
CIO	Chief information officer
CtoG	Citizen-to-government
DPADM	Division for Public Administration and Development Management
ECOSOC	United Nations Economic and Social Council
ESCs	Economic and Social Councils
FOI	Freedom of information
FOIA	Freedom of information acts
GtoC	Government-to-citizen
HIV/AIDS	Human immunodeficiency virus/acquired immune deficiency syndrome
ICT	Information and communications technology
IGF	Internet Governance Forum
IT	Information technology
IUCN	International Union for Conservation of Nature
MDGs	Millennium Development Goals
OAG	Office of the Auditor General (of Canada)
SAI	Supreme audit institution
SDGs	Sustainable Development Goals
UN	United Nations
UNCSD	United Nations Conference on Sustainable Development

UNDESA	United Nations Department of Economic and Social Affairs
UNDP	United Nations Development Programme
UNPACS	United Nations Public Administration Country Studies
UNPAN	United Nations Public Administration Network
UNPSA	United Nations Public Service Awards
WPSR	World Public Sector Report

Contents

Chapter 1
Governance, a priority for development   1

Chapter 2
Responsive governance   25

Boxes

Charts

Figures

Chapter 1

Governance, a priority for development

1. A review of governance, development and the state

In August 2015, United Nations Member States reached an agreement on the outcome document that will constitute the Agenda for Sustainable Development—the development framework beyond the Millennium Development Goals (MDGs) target date. At the request of General Assembly, the Secretary-General gave a report that synthesized the full range of inputs as a contribution to the intergovernmental negotiations in the lead up to the Summit on Sustainable Development to be held in New York in September 2015. This synthesis report[4] underscored the importance of strengthening effective, accountable, participatory and inclusive governance among key elements required for implementing a universal agenda for the next 15 years.

The 2015 WPSR seeks to contribute to this discussion from a public governance perspective. It focuses on responsive and accountable public governance as cross-cutting enablers of development. The report begins with the premise that the new development agenda will require responsive and accountable governance at national and subnational levels in all countries for the goals to be achieved. People are at the centre of responsive and accountable public governance. They all rely upon the State to readjust its roles to include an enhanced focus on the needs of citizens, especially in the protection of fundamental freedoms and rights and effective and efficient delivery of essential services.

Today, the term "governance" is used in different contexts. At geopolitical levels, for instance, it is used to characterize global governance, national governance, local governance, and so on. It is used in various public spheres including economic governance, social governance and environmental governance. It is used to describe various global or public goods such as land governance, water governance and internet governance. And it may refer to various economic sectors such as public governance, and corporate governance.

This publication focuses on public governance, or "the exercise of economic, political and administrative authority to manage a country's affairs at

---

4   United Nations General Assembly, "The road to dignity by 2030: ending poverty, transforming all lives and protecting the planet", synthesis report of the Secretary-General on the post-2015 sustainable development agenda, A/69/700, 4 December 2014, para. 50, p. 11.

all levels. ...", which as presented later in this chapter, has evolved as a concept.[5] Though commonly used, the term "(public) governance"[6] itself carries no uni versally accepted definition. It is used in various dimensions and contexts.[7]

The 2015 World Public Sector Report (WPSR) also draws on the deliberations of the 12th session of the United Nations Committee of Experts on Public Administration (CEPA) which focused on the role of responsive and accountable governance in the new development agenda.[8] As shown later in this Report, responsiveness and accountability are two fundamental principles of governance which are analyzed in view of their key role as cross-cutting enablers of development.

The advent of the modern nation State, or a geopolitical territory under one government, is the manifestation of a vision of governance that balances political decision-making and the administration of public affairs. CEPA defined the "public sector" as that segment of the economy, that comprises of persons and organizations engaged in the delivery of public goods and services to citizens.[9]

The state plays a key role in development. However, in many developing countries, the capacity of the State itself needs strengthening to be an effective enabler of development.

It "is increasingly being acknowledged that the state is a key actor in the development process. ... states, [as political institutions] can either guarantee

---

5   See United Nations, "Public Administration Glossary", definition and explanatory note for "governance". Available from www.unpan.org/Directories/UNPublic AdministrationGlossary/tabid/928/language/en-US/Default.aspx.

6   The term has its origin in the Greek language, κυβερναω, and it refers to steering. Steering, for example a ship, is not only a matter of keeping the ship afloat and in forward, backward or sideways motion. It strongly demands knowledge of the direction and ensuring that the ship is constantly on course in that direction. See also www. unpan.org/Directories/UNPublicAdministrationGlossary/tabid/928/language/en-US/Default.aspx.

7   At geo-political levels, for instance, the term governance is used to characterize global governance, national governance, and local governance. It is used in different public spheres including economic governance, social governance, and environmental governance. It is used to deal with different global commons or public goods such as land governance, water governance, and internet governance. And it may refer to different economic sectors such as public governance and corporate governance.

8   See www.unpan.org/DPADM/CEPA/12thSession/tabid/1544/language/en-US/ Default.aspx. The United Nations Committee of Experts on Public Administration, established by the Economic and Social Council (ECOSOC) in its resolution 2001/45, comprises 24 members who meet annually at UN Headquarters in New York. The Committee is responsible for supporting the work of ECOSOC that concerns the promotion and development of public administration and governance among Member States in connection with the UN Millennium Development Goals.

9   See United Nations, "Public Administration Glossary", definition for "governance", "public sector" and "public goods and services". Available from www.unpan.org/ DPADM/ProductsServices/Glossary/tabid/1395/language/en-US/Default.aspx.

people's freedom and a measure of social justice, or can hold back development. In the economic sphere, how the public sector is structured, administered and operated, as well as what policies are pursued, has a great impact on people's well-being."[10] However, the state, through the government as its executive arm, is not the only actor. Private sector and civil society play important roles in development alongside the public sector.

Since 1948, the United Nations has been supporting Member States, especially developing countries, to develop their state capacities to govern effectively and respond to challenges in their pursuit of economic and social development.[11] The diversity of challenges becomes more pronounced when it comes to those related to public governance. States are responsible for maintaining peace and security; upholding constitutionalism and the rule of law; ensuring fair, accessible and affordable justice for all; ensuring respect for human rights; promoting popular participation and institutions of local governance; providing effective delivery of essential services; and ultimately creating and sustaining trust and legitimacy of state institutions.

Despite economic advances, many countries in all regions still face challenges in carrying out their state responsibilities. For instance, how can states ensure public security? How can they ensure access to justice for all including the poor and disadvantaged groups? How can they protect the citizens' most fundamental rights, equally for men and women, and enhance social, economic, cultural and political inclusion? Other challenges include enhancing the effectiveness of representative bodies at central and subnational levels to perform their democratic functions; addressing socioeconomic inequality and economic stagnation; effectively fighting corruption, drugs and crime; bringing about transparent, accountable and inclusive state-citizen partnerships for effective service delivery as well as greater and more efficient intercountry development cooperation.

It is clear that the state is called upon to play a key role in development. However, in many developing countries, the capacity of the state itself needs strengthening to be an effective enabler of development. Progressively, the challenges facing the development of public governance capacity have included understanding the changes in the concepts and practices of public governance. As explained below, one could argue that there has been a conceptual evolution in the field of governance. This can be summarized as a cumulative paradigm shift from public administration to public management to public governance.[12]

Public administration is indispensable to responsive and accountable governance and development in general. It serves as the bedrock of the rule of law and effective delivery of essential public services.

---

10 World Public Sector Report 2001: Globalization and the State, (United Nations publication, Sales No.: E.01.II.H.2), p. iii.

11 United Nations General Assembly resolution 246 (III): International facilities for the promotion of training in public administration, A/Res/246(III), 4 December 1948.

12 United Nations, "From public administration to governance: the paradigm shift in the link between government and citizens", 2005.

Public administration is a structure and practice, a concept and a paradigm. As a structure and practice, it is based upon a legitimate and rational set of rules with delegated legal authority. It depends on the expertise, impartiality, integrity and professionalism of public administrators who provide continuous, predictable and standardized public services in the public interest. As an effective instrument of the state,[13] it is expected to be the basis for human security and development. It is indispensable to responsive and accountable governance and development in general, because it serves as the bedrock of the rule of law and effective delivery of essential public services.

However, in the latter part of the 1970s, along with criticism of the practice of public administration, there was a call for a more prominent role for private enterprise in development. The critics claimed that public administrative practices paid too much attention to the rules, regulations, controls, procedures and processes at the expense of providing effective services to the public. They were blamed for red tape, sluggishness, insensitivity to public needs, wasteful utilization of public resources, undue focus on process and procedure rather than on results and so on. Thus, in many countries, public administration, as a paradigm and a practice, came to be viewed negatively as a burden on the taxpayer.[14]

A new school of thought on public administration called "public management" emerged. According to this new school of thought, managing public affairs would best be performed through the application of private enterprise management principles and practices. Efficiency in the utilization of resources, effectiveness of results, customer focus and a reliance on market forces, especially in matters of economic decisions, were stressed. Increasing the role and influence of the private sector called for rolling back the frontiers of the state. In effect, there was a push for minimizing the size of the public sector and narrowing the field of operations of public administration.

But in the 1990s, the delivery of public services and public goods were observed to deteriorate.[15] This deterioration was attributed to too much emphasis on efficiency, based on private sector management approaches in the running of public affairs. Some goods and services could not be adequately provided through a strict adherence to the practices and dictates of market forces. An emphasis on market-led development did not achieve the desired economic and social progress. In many cases, it led to greater social inequalities without

---

13 Jean-Louis Quermonne, "L'appareil administratif de l'Etat", (Editions du Seuil, Paris, 1991).

14 United Nations, "From public administration to governance: the paradigm shift in the link between government and citizens", 2005.

15 United Nations, Committee of Experts on Public Administration, Revitalizing Public Administration as a Strategic Action for Sustainable Human Development: an Overview, E/C.16/2004/2, 2004.

strong State leadership for more socially inclusive policies. In other words, governments needed to be backed by strong public institutions with responsibility for guaranteeing the public interest over private ones.

Lapses in regulation and controls provided avenues for increased corruption in public offices; private sector practices in management of human resources, such as introducing short-term contracts over career appointments, eroded commitment to public service values. Ultimately, the public did not get better services as expected. It became apparent that the market forces did not necessarily always decide in favour of the public interest.[16] Nor did they always involve the public in deciding, planning, implementing, monitoring and evaluating government action. Ensuring that the interest and needs of citizens remained at the centre of government action requires searching for ways to strengthen citizens' roles and give the citizens a voice to influence the way public managers planned and implemented the State's functions.

Therefore, public institutions could not simply revert to conventional bureaucratic functions. The concept of governance emerged to emphasize the participation and interests of the public as well as the need for public officials to uphold strong responsiveness, equity, transparency and accountability as core principles of public management.

It is now clear that the term "public governance" has become closely associated with the way the State plays its various roles in social, political and economic development. The practice of managing public affairs encompasses aspects that are related to the concepts of public administration, public management and public governance. The three have merged to complement one another in the management of the State and development. By the end of the 20th century, it was clear that the way forward would be through cross-sector partnerships among governments, private businesses and civil society organizations in achieving good governance.[17] It became essential, therefore, for governments to incorporate frameworks and mechanisms that would facilitate greater participation in policy formulation by all governance actors to enhance responsiveness and accountability in the management of public affairs. ◆

The concept of governance emphasizes the participation and interest of the public as well as strong responsiveness, equity, transparency and accountability of public officials at the centre of public management.

---

16 Ibid.

17 See United Nations, "Public Administration Glossary", definition for "good governance". Available from www.unpan.org/DPADM/ProductsServices/Glossary/tabid/1395/language/en-US/Default.aspx.

2. Public leadership in people-centred development

Responsive and accountable public governance begins with the State leadership working with the citizens to formulate and agree on a vision for the country that will guide the development efforts focused on the well-being of the people. World leaders of the Member States clearly demonstrated this in September 2000 in New York through the United Nations Millennium Declaration.[18] The United Nations Millennium Declaration heralded the formulation of a ground-breaking global vision for improving lives in the new millennium. Its implementation was formulated in the eight Millennium Development Goals (MDGs) that have been, in many ways, at the centre of development efforts in many countries.

Lessons from MDG implementation include: emphasis on responsive public leadership, inclusive growth, decent employment and social protection; and the need to allocate more resources to ensure universal access to essential services.

The MDGs and associated targets gave concrete shape and measurable results to this vision. They aim to achieve human development through the eradication of poverty and hunger; improvements in education, health, gender equality, environment sustainability and the promotion of global partnerships. The Millennium Declaration also emphasized human rights, democracy and good governance. Together, the MDGs embodied global and national development priorities for the period from 2000 to 2015. The formulation of the MDGs demonstrated a critical fact in responsive public governance. Responsive public leadership is critical in determining the vision for a country's development. This role is best taken up with involvement of the people in order to make the development focused on their current and future needs.

With the MDGs, "What was new was the sense of possibility—the conviction that through a combination of targets, tangible investments, genuine action and political will, countries and people working together could end poverty in all its forms".[19] As a result, in developing regions, the proportion of people living on less than $1.25 a day decreased from 47 per cent in 1990 to 22 per cent in 2010. The number of children who were not attending primary school fell from 102 million in 2000 to 58 million in 2012. The worldwide mortality rate of children under five dropped by almost 50 per cent between 1990 and 2012. Over the past 12 years, over 200 million slum dwellers benefited from improved water and sanitation facilities, durable housing or sufficient living space.[20] These are but a few illustrations of achieving or making rapid progress towards the MDGs.

---

18   United Nations, A/RES/55/2.

19   United Nations, The Millennium Development Goals Report 2014, p. 9.

20   Ibid.

Emphasizing responsive public leadership, inclusive growth, decent employment and social protection as well as allocating more resources for essential services and ensuring access for all are among the lessons learned. Steering all governance stakeholders towards consensus on such development policies and public services is a unique role of governments. Any government outreach should benefit from inclusive public engagement frameworks as well as citizen-driven initiatives and people's willingness to participate in decision-making.

The United Nations Conference on Sustainable Development (Rio +20), held in Rio de Janeiro, Brazil in 2012, once again demonstrated how key responsive public leadership is to visioning for development. This time, unlike in 2000 when they set the MDGs, the world leaders made a critical improvement. The voices of the people were included in the meeting.

More than 40,000 people attended Rio+20. The outcome document, "The future we want", adopted at the conference, called for greening the economy, promoting corporate sustainability reporting, assessing well-being beyond gross domestic product, financing sustainable development, tackling sustainable consumption and production, focusing on improving gender equity and reducing inequality, among other wide-ranging actions. There was a call for sustainable development goals (SDGs) to be integrated into the United Nations 2030 Agenda for Sustainable Development. Again, the Member States "recogniz(ed) that effective governance at the local, subnational, national, regional and global levels representing the voices and interests of all is critical for advancing sustainable development".[21]

In 2013, to implement the Rio+20 outcome, the General Assembly established the Open Working Group on SDGs and the Intergovernmental Committee of Experts on Sustainable Development Financing. The first body developed a set of SDGs for consideration by the General Assembly; the second proposed options for financing mechanisms in the context of the new sustainable development agenda.

Facilitating the development, transfer and dissemination of clean and environmentally sound technologies; setting the incentives for sustainable consumption and production; and promoting intergenerational solidarity are among the challenges of sustainable development.[22] The success of mainstreaming the concept of sustainable development, implementing consistent policies and mobilizing appropriate resources will take a responsive State and accountable mechanisms for strengthening governance. ◆

An innovative State and responsive and accountable governance are needed for the success of mainstreaming sustainable development initiatives and mobilizing appropriate resources.

---

21 United Nations, The Future We Want (A/CONF.216/1.1), 2012, para. 76.

22 See Implementation of Agenda 21, the Programme for the Further Implementation of Agenda 21 and the outcomes of the World Summit on Sustainable Development and of the United Nations Conference on Sustainable Development (A/68/321).

3. Responsive and accountable governance and the 2030 Agenda for Sustainable Development

Responsive and accountable govern-ance engages the people in decision-making, implemen-tation, monitoring and evaluation. It responds to people's needs and is open to people's inputs and scrutiny.

The MDGs provided opportunities for observing what worked and what did not work well in their implementation. While monitoring progress towards the MDGs, world leaders have become more aware that "responsive and account-able governance" are a prerequisite to successful development policies and effective delivery of essential public services. As the international community is about to adopt the 2030 Agenda for Sustainable Development, the impor-tance of accountable institutions and responsive decision-making at all levels are considered important factors of the new framework.[23]

Responsive and accountable governance engages the people in the pro-cesses of decision- and policymaking, implementation, monitoring and evalu-ation. It focuses plans and action of public leadership and government on the needs of the people and involves them in identifying those needs. It provides access to public information, constantly listens to the people and ensures that government and its agencies are open to people's inputs and scrutiny. Most importantly, it develops institutions, structures, systems and practices that pro-mote and support the involvement and participation of the people and ensure equal access to services by all.

The High-Level Panel of Eminent Persons on the Post-2015 Develop-ment Agenda, set up by the United Nations Secretary-General in July 2012, reported, "people the world over expect their governments to be honest, accountable, and responsive to their needs. We are calling for a fundamen-tal shift—to recognize peace and good governance as core elements of well being, not optional extras."[24] As mentioned earlier in this chapter, prior to the High-Level Panel's report, CEPA also focused on the importance of the role of responsive and accountable governance in achieving the Millennium Develop-

---

23 Outcome Document, Open Working Group for Sustainable Development Goals, 16.6 and 16.7, Sustainable Development Knowledge Platform: http://sustainable development.un.org/focussdgs.html.

24 Report of the High-Level Panel of Eminent Persons on the Post-2015 Development Agenda 2013, (E/2013/44–E/C.16/2013/6), Executive Summary. Available from http://report.post2015hlp.org/digital-report-executive-summary.html.

ment Goals (MDGs) and the new development agenda.[25] In 2014, CEPA also referred to "transparent, participatory and accountable governance" among the "foundations for sustainable development".[26]

Responsiveness and accountability draw attention to the centrality of the social contract between the state and citizens. That is, states need to respond to the real needs of the people and be accountable for their decisions and actions to them. Citizens should fulfil their part of the contract by participating in democratic processes, contributing to taxes and generally participating in civic life.

In 2012, the United Nations System Task Team on the Post-2015 United Nations Development Agenda observed, "Recent events in the Arab States ... underscore the importance of addressing democratic governance[27] deficits at the national and sub-national levels to ensure the legitimacy of development policies and to support the empowerment of people".[28] Moreover, an Expert Group Meeting held in 2012 in the Arab region concluded, "... the public sector must undergo reform to build the trust of citizens in government and public services .... The extensive challenges facing the region cannot be tackled alone. The public sector must be willing to solicit the assistance and cooperation of civil society, the private sector, think tanks and the international community (including the UN) if it is to succeed in its development goals".[29]

These events emphasize the need for a new social contract that requires giving more space for citizens to express their preferences and for governments

---

25 See www.unpan.org/DPADM/CEPA/12thSession/tabid/1544/language/en-US/ Default.aspx. The United Nations Committee of Experts on Public Administration, established by the Economic and Social Council (ECOSOC) in its resolution 2001/45, comprises 24 members who meet annually at UN Headquarters in New York. The Committee is responsible for supporting the work of ECOSOC that concerns the promotion and development of public administration and governance among Member States, in connection with the UN Millennium Development Goals.

26 United Nations, Report on the 13th Session of the Committee of Experts on Public Administration, New York, 7-11 April, 2014 (see E/2014/44-E/C.16/2014/6). Available from http://workspace.unpan.org/sites/Internet/Documents/UNPAN92994. pdf.

27 See United Nations, "Public Administration Glossary", E/C.16/2006/4 definition for "democratic governance". Available from www.unpan.org/DPADM/Products Services/Glossary/tabid/1395/language/en-US/Default.aspx.

28 "Realizing the future we want for all". UN System Task Team on the Post-2015 UN Development Agenda Report to the Secretary-General, June 2012, para. 49.

29 See details of the Expert Group Meeting on Citizen Engagement and Post-2015 Development Agenda, Beirut, 3-4 December 2012. Available from www.unpan. org/Events/BrowseEventsbyCalendar/tabid/94/mctl/EventDetails/ModuleID/1532/ ItemID/2270/language/en-US/Default.aspx?selecteddate=12/3/2012.

to better account for their decisions and actions. Consequently, there is a need to reconceptualize the way responsibility and accountability are shared among governments, the private sector and civil society organizations for formulating development strategies and delivering essential services. This report aims to contribute to advancing this thinking.

In reviewing the MDG framework, the United Nations System Task Team noted that a major strength is its focus on a limited set of concrete, common human development goals and targets. However, the deliberate decision to focus on a few goals also resulted in not adequately addressing other dimensions of development such as peace and security, governance, the rule of law and human rights. A more inclusive consultation perhaps could have resulted in a framework also encompassing these priorities for development. The next chapters of the 2015 WPSR illustrate why responsive and accountable processes in public governance are important priorities in the new period of development, especially in implementing the SDGs.

CEPA stressed the multidimensional nature of governance. "In the context of the post-2015 discussion, a good balance of political/institutional and managerial/technical aspects of governance would be needed. While technical approaches, such as open government, were essential to producing good outcomes, it should be noted that the institutional aspects of governance were key to sustaining principles and values of democracy".[30]

The next section touches on some of the challenges that need to be addressed through responsive and accountable governance in the process of development. ◆

---

30 See http://www.unpan.org/DPADM/CEPA/12thSession/tabid/1544/language/en-US/Default.aspx.

4. Development challenges of environmental protection, extreme poverty eradication, and people empowerment

Various forums in the run-up to 2015 identified numerous challenges to responsive and accountable governance and for sustainable development. For instance, the United Nations Secretary-General's High-Level Panel on Global Sustainability asked:

"But what, then, is to be done if we are to make a real difference for the world's people and the planet? We must grasp the dimensions of the challenge. We must recognize that the drivers of that challenge include unsustainable lifestyles, production and consumption patterns and the impact of population growth. As the global population grows from 7 billion to almost 9 billion by 2040, and the number of middle-class consumers increases by 3 billion over the next 20 years, the demand for resources will rise exponentially. By 2030, the world will need at least 50 per cent more food, 45 per cent more energy and 30 per cent more water—all at a time when environmental boundaries are throwing up new limits to supply. This is true not least for climate change, which affects all aspects of human and planetary health".[31]

The Panel called for a new political economy and democratic governance for sustainable development. It noted that environmental devastation needs to be stopped through the coherent action of both governments and corporations. All levels and actors of governance need to embrace sustainable development for the future. All levels of governments need to move from silo mentalities to integrated policymaking.

All levels and actors of governance need to embrace sustainable development as the future.

The United Nations High-Level Panel of Eminent Persons on the Post-2015 Development Agenda noted the progress made on the MDGs by the international community and concluded:

"Given this remarkable success, it would be a mistake to simply tear up the MDGs and start from scratch. As world leaders agreed at Rio in 2012, new goals and targets need to be grounded in respect for universal human rights, and finish the job that the MDGs started. Central to this is eradicating extreme

31 United Nations Secretary-General's High-Level Panel on Global Sustainability (2012). "Resilient people, resilient planet: a future worth choosing", Overview. New York: United Nations., para. 7, available from http://uscib.org/docs/GSPReport Overview_A4%20size.pdf.

poverty from the face of the earth by 2030. This is something that leaders have promised time and again throughout history. Today, it can actually be done".[32]

Building peace and effective, open and accountable institutions for all is one of the five big, transformative shifts needed for a universal, new agenda.

This Panel called for five big transformative shifts for a universal sustainable development agenda: 1) leave no one behind; 2) put sustainable development at the core; 3) transform economies for jobs and inclusive growth; 4) build peace and effective, open and accountable institutions for all; and 5) forge a new global partnership.

In addition, the United Nations Commission on Social Development deliberated on the priority theme of promoting empowerment of people in achieving poverty eradication, social integration and full employment and decent work for all at its 51st Session in 2013. It stated:

"Looking forward, sustainable poverty reduction can only be achieved with the active participation of people affected by poverty. However, inequitable power relations inhibit the participation of men and women living in poverty. The lack of social, political and economic opportunities available to people living in poverty constrain their potential to improve their lives. As a result, people living in poverty often feel powerless to improve their position. It is people's own actions that empower them, rather than those of others. However, governments, civil society organizations and other development partners can support the empowerment of people by reducing—or removing—the barriers that constrain their opportunities and by ensuring that initiatives and programmes aimed at reducing poverty are participatory".[33]

The concrete measures that the Commission identified as enabling people's empowerment include: 1) social policies addressing specific needs of disadvantaged social groups; 2) people-centred development as a core objective of social and sustainable development; 3) more comprehensive, integrated inclusive policies and programmes that aim to improve access and opportunities for all; 4) strengthening the capacity of institutions facilitating the participation and engagement of citizens so that they become more efficient, effective, transparent and accountable; 5) ensuring access to justice and legal instruments to reduce/eliminate poverty and inequality; and 6) promoting inclusive and

---

32 Report of the High-Level Panel of Eminent Persons on the Post-2015 Development Agenda 2013. Available from http://report.post2015hlp.org/digital-report-executive-summary.html.

33 Promoting empowerment of people in achieving poverty eradication, social integration and full employment and decent work for all, Report of the Secretary General, (E/CN.5/2013/3), para. 23.

sustainable labour markets, social protection and investments.[34] The report of the 52nd session also stressed that,

"Special efforts should be made to foster the participation of all people, including women, people living in poverty and those belonging to disadvantaged and vulnerable groups, including children, youth, older persons, persons with disabilities and indigenous peoples, in all aspects of political, economic, social, civic and cultural life, in particular the planning, implementation, monitoring and evaluation, as appropriate, of policies that affect them".[35]

On the one hand, rising to deal with the complex development challenges and integrating responses to economic, social and environmental problems expand the reach of public governance and its relevance. On the other hand, traditional hierarchical processes for decision-making and centralized responsibility and accountability can impede public service responsiveness. The United Nations Committee of Experts on Public Administration recommended:

"A critical post-2015 role for Members States of the United Nations is to ensure clarity in the respective roles, responsibilities and resources of the main stakeholders, which include not only government at the national and local levels but also civil society, the private sector, donors and other major actors".[36]

The Secretary-General's synthesis report on the new sustainable development agenda also emphasized the importance of a shared responsibility for the successful attainment of development goals. The report, in particular, stated: "If we are to succeed, the new agenda cannot remain the exclusive domain of institutions and governments. It must be embraced by people". [37] ◆

---

34 Agenda item 3a, priority theme: Promoting empowerment of people in achieving poverty eradication, social integration and full employment and decent work for all, Chair's Summary. Available from www.un.org/esa/socdev/csocd/2013/summaries/ Chairssummaryofdiscussionsonprioritytheme.pdf.

35 United Nations, Commission on Social Development, Report on the 52nd Session, E/2014/26-E/CN.5/2014/10, 2014.

36 Committee of Experts on Public Administration, Report on the 12th Session, New York 15-19 April 2013 (E/2013/44-E/C.16/2013/6), para. 62. Available from www. unpan.org/DPADM/CEPA/12thSession/tabid/1544/language/en-US/Default.aspx.

37 United Nations General Assembly, "The road to dignity by 2030: ending poverty, transforming all lives and protecting the planet", Synthesis report of the Secretary-General on the post-2015 sustainable development agenda, A/69/700, 4 December 2014, para. 132, p. 27.

5. Governance challenges of institutional coherence, multi-stakeholder engagement, and harnessing the potential of the Internet and mobile technology

The experiences of developing countries and countries with transitioning economies, set out important challenges for designing governance reforms, particularly for achieving long-lasting development. Some of these challenges, addressed by the United Nations WPSR since its inception, include:

- Harnessing information, communications technology (ICT) through a national strategy is needed in order to benefit from and reduce the risks of globalization.[38] Addressing globalization challenges, including the need for the State to become a "learning organization".

- Harnessing ICT, which by itself will not result in a different or better government, nor a higher quality of life. Nonetheless, thoughtful e-government reform should be a tool for creating public value.[39]

- Unlocking the human potential for public sector performance as the lifeblood and strength of the public service. Strengthening the capacity of national public administration is one of the best measures that developing countries can undertake to attain development goals.[40]

- Governance challenges from the perspective of deepening socio-economic development. Supporting, enlarging and deepening civic engagement requires making ongoing initiatives more participatory and inclusive. It further requires institutional adjustments, free access to information, capacity-building and political commitment.[41]

---

38 United Nations, "Globalization and the state", World Public Sector Report, ST/ESA/PAD/SER.26, 2001.

39 United Nations, "E-Government at the crossroads", World Public Sector Report, ST/ESA/PAD/ER.E/49, 2003.

40 United Nations, "Unlocking the human potential for public sector performance", World Public Sector Report, ST/ESA/PAD/SER.E/63, 2005.

41 United Nations, "People matter: civic engagement in public governance", World Public Sector Report, ST/ESA/PAD/SER.E/108, 2008.

- Reconstructing public administration after conflict, in contexts plagued by social upheaval, diminished security, damaged infra-structure, reduced productive capacity, revenue shortfalls and weakened human resources. This has more chance to succeed when the public administration earns the trust of the people through effectively providing essential services.[42]

The report of the 13th session of CEPA in 2014 reaffirmed that "good governance and the rule of law at the national and international levels are essential for sustained, inclusive and equitable economic growth, sustainable development and the eradication of poverty and hunger".[43] The emphasis on the importance of peace, good governance, the rule of law and human rights seems higher in the discussions on the SDGs than it was in the discourse on MDGs.[44] This report affirms that with a movement towards development that is rights-based and governance that is democratic and participatory, govern-ance responsiveness and accountability will be central factors in implementing the new development outcomes.

Governance respon-siveness and account-ability will be central factors in reaching sustainable develop-ment outcomes.

In addition to the challenges previously dealt with by the WPSR, among the main challenges of responsive and accountable governance is insti-tutional coherence for sustainable development. Coherence has several dimen-sions, including aligning formal and informal institutions; creating synergies among economic, social and environmental institutions, and empowering local institutions on the principle of subsidiarity from among other levels. There has to be also coherence and "integrity between the implementation process and governance goals".[45] The challenge is that "implementers need to engage with all stakeholders, take account of responses, problem solve and influence toward their desired outcome; simply issuing an instruction may achieve a degree of compliance"[46] which is different from attaining a long lasting result.

Formal institutions are rules that are directly or indirectly enforced by the State, such as electoral rules, the rules of separation of powers, the

---

42 United Nations, "Reconstructing public administration after conflict: challeng-es, practices and lessons learned", World Public Sector Report, ST/ESA/PAD/SER.E/135, 2010.

43 United Nations, Report on the 13th Session of the Committee of Experts on Public Administration, New York, 7-11 April 2014 (see E/2014/44-E/C.16/2014/6). Avail-able from http://workspace.unpan.org/sites/Internet/Documents/UNPAN92994.pdf.

44 Outcome Document, Open Working Group for Sustainable Development, Introduc-tion, para. 12 and goal 4.7, Sustainable Development Knowledge Platform: http://sustainabledevelopment.un.org/focussdgs.html.

45 Margaret Saner, Contribution to World Public Sector Brief 2013.

46 Ibid., p. 6.

specification of rights of citizens, among others. In each case, there are laws, regulations and legal judgements that define the appropriate rules and the enforcement of these rules. Informal institutions refer to all other types of rules and their enforcement processes. Individuals and organizations are always following many "rules" of behaviour in their interactions that are not rules defined or enforced by the state. Responsive and accountable governance to eradicate extreme poverty, a highly complex and contextual problem, needs to align reforms to both formal and informal institutions. For example, a government may tackle poverty through implementing formal social safety nets and encouraging informal community mutual-aid schemes.

Responsive and accountable governance not only builds institutional capacity but includes leadership that respects and safeguards institutions.

Institutions have been created for political, economic, social and other purposes. Many of the formal development institutions have been configured for economic development. The question of whether they can adapt to the need to integrate the economic with social and environmental realities of sustainable development remains to be answered. States will also have to be able to implement reforms of formal institutions that take into account the informal characteristics of societies. Moreover, they will do so by being aware that responsive and accountable governance goes beyond merely building capacity of institutions. It includes leadership that respects and safeguards institutions.

In addition to integrating horizontally among different sectors, the institutional framework should also harmonize actions vertically among the different levels of government. The principle of subsidiarity, or the idea that a central authority should have a subsidiary function, performing only those tasks which cannot be performed effectively at a more immediate or local level,[47] should decentralize responsibilities and resources to local authorities. At Rio+20, the Member States underlined the need for "more coherent and integrated planning and decision-making at the national, subnational and local levels as appropriate" and, to this end, they called "on countries to strengthen national, subnational and/or local institutions or relevant multi-stakeholder bodies and processes, as appropriate, dealing with sustainable development, including to coordinate on matters of sustainable development and to enable effective integration of the three dimensions of sustainable development".[48] This also shows "the need to become more sensitive to local variation and ambitions. National and international agendas are significant in making progress on sustainable development and can be informed and enhanced by a deeper understanding of the impact and relevance of local concerns and agendas".[49]

---

47 See United Nations, "Public Administration Glossary", definition for "subsidiarity". Available from www.unpan.org/Directories/UNPublicAdministrationGlossary/ tabid/928/language/en-US/Default.aspx.

48 United Nations, The Future We Want (A/CONF.216/1.1), 2012, para. 101.

49 Margaret Saner, Contribution to World Public Sector Brief 2013.

In Rio+20, the Member States recognized "… the important role that … authorities and communities can play in implementing sustainable development, including by engaging citizens and stakeholders and providing them with relevant information, as appropriate, on the three dimensions of sustainable development". They further acknowledged "the importance of involving all relevant decision makers in the planning and implementation of sustainable development policies".[50] Follow-up international consultations on the 2030 Agenda for Sustainable Development have engaged a broad range of stakeholders. For example, in 2013, the United Nations Development Programme and the Office of the United Nations High Commissioner for Human Rights were co-leaders of a consultative process in collaboration with representatives from civil society organizations, and multi-stakeholder meetings. The process also included representatives from local and international civil society, governments, the private sector, international and multilateral institutions, academia and non-affiliated individuals from around the world. Similar multi-stakeholder consultations are taking place at the national and subnational levels.

Citizen engagement and public participation that involves all stakeholders can increase not only more accurate problem definition and solution generation but also ownership and public accountability. The governance challenge is to identify those issues that best lend themselves to wide public consultation and inclusive decision-making as well as the optimal levels and modalities of consultation. For instance, national security serves as an example where consultation may not be advisable due to the need to protect sensitive information. Conversely, consultation may be advisable for instance when to reduce health costs, a government decides to close one of the two only hospitals, each serving a different part of the geographical area in a rural community. Without a clear participation strategy, appropriation by elites or special interest groups can take place. In the latter example, the competitive process of voicing concerns by each of the two sides can lead to a decision based on the most powerful voice represented during the consultation process.

ICT has contributed to achieving many of the MDGs. However, with more than two-thirds of those in developing countries remaining unconnected, the digital divide must be bridged if ICT is to enable the tools that will be used to achieve the new sustainable development goals. ICT provides a platform to better integrate and accelerate delivery on all three pillars of sustainable development—economic, social and environmental. But ICT alone cannot guarantee development without an enabling environment. Access to broadband, Internet governance and cybersecurity measures must be developed in order to safeguard online security, freedoms and respect for human rights.

ICT provides a platform to better integrate and accelerate delivery on all three pillars of sustainable development.

---

50 United Nations, "Rio+20 United Nations Conference on Sustainable Development." Outcome of the Conference: The future we want Brazil, June 20-22, 2012 (A/CONF/216/L.1), 2012, paras. 42 and 43.

If responsive and accountable governance has to be promoted as a matter of priority in order to achieve the new development agenda, traditional approaches to reform may not be enough. Rather, Member States may have to undertake transformations in the institutional arrangements and practices of public governance. Knowing that the exact nature of the transformations required will differ by country and its needs, the following chapters will analyse policy options to strengthen governance responsiveness and accountability. However, it is important to state in advance that the transformations required in each different context are difficult to ascertain at an aggregate level. ◆

6. Lessons from Millennium Development Goals: from reform to transformation

The evolution in the collective vision of development in the intervening decade or so between the MDGs and the SDGs is characterized by integration. At the level of individual welfare, the unfinished business of poverty eradication of the MDGs integrates not only meeting basic physical needs but also increasing overall psychological well-being. At the national and international levels of development, the vision integrates inclusive economic growth, social justice and environmental sustainability. At the normative level, the vision integrates the United Nations mandates of peace and security, sustainable development and the respect for human rights.

The 17 SDGs represent a shift towards a development that is people-centred and rights-based with greater inclusiveness and participatory decision-making. They "constitute an integrated, indivisible set of global priorities for sustainable development" and "seek to complete the unfinished business of the MDGs and respond to new challenges".[51]

Responsive and accountable governance is a key enabler as well as an integral part of this vision of sustainable development. Addressing the challenges related to the three pillars of sustainable development will require the

---

51 United Nations, Outcome Document, Open Working Group for Sustainable Development, Introduction, para. 18, Sustainable Development Knowledge Platform: http://sustainabledevelopment.un.org/focussdgs.html.

development of adequate institutional, human, financial and material capacities in government and governance as a whole. SDG 16, in particular, calls for promoting peaceful and inclusive societies for sustainable development; providing access to justice for all; and building effective, accountable and inclusive institutions at all levels.

The nature of the development and governance challenges facing the world for the new development agenda calls for not only reform but transformation of the public sector and public administration. The 12th Session of the United Nations Committee of Experts on Public Administration made recommendations on seven key areas as essential components for enhancing responsive and accountable public governance helpful to the attainment of the SDGs: 1) access to information; 2) innovation in governance to avoid becoming trapped in administrative routine; 3) combining the global and local, avoiding a "one size fits all" approach and using indicators that fit the shifting socioeconomic conditions of a country; 4) quality, relevance and local proximity of data; 5) local ownership of development objectives and some combination of horizontal and top-down engagement in setting objectives; 6) the role of the political system, including the importance of political competition and inclusion for longer-term development objectives; and 7) searching for good local practices and learning to scale them up.

First, access to public information is essential for participatory governance and is a vital first step in promoting citizen engagement in public policy decision-making processes. Access to public information is also a prerequisite for democratic governance and social inclusion. Citizens need to be enabled and encouraged to participate in defining public problems that affect their lives. Public agencies can play a critical role in public problem definition through the synthesis and dissemination of multiple perspectives. This approach helps governments to design responsive policies, and by effectively implementing them, governments enhance their legitimacy.

Second, innovation in governance can prevent stagnation in public administration. The need exists in many countries for more modern administrative processes. The scope for innovations in public governance was notably enhanced by ICT in the past three decades. ICT empowers innovations for connectivity between governments and their constituents. These systems enable public organizations to standardize responses and achieve equality in their communications and interactions with citizens, as much as they enable customization and flexible processes. They help public administrations to guard against the perpetuation of bureaucratic regimentation that could render public agencies irresponsive and ineffective. Innovations are not limited to ICT alone. They can be found in institutional configurations, service delivery mechanisms and social innovations. Throughout the past decade, the United Nations Public Service Awards (UNPSA) programme has provided incentives for innovation in public agencies. Many excellent strategies have been documented in case studies available through the United Nations Public Administration Network at www.UNPAN.org.

Frameworks for performance measurement and evaluation have gained momentum in the past decade for their potential to guide performance management.

Third, international and regional agreements have fostered connectivity at the global level and facilitated the diffusion of best practices and lessons learned. Countries have opportunities to replicate these or adapt them to suit their particular requirements. For the public sector, public performance management is essential to monitoring improvements. Frameworks for performance measurement and evaluation have gained momentum in the past decade for their potential to guide performance management. Previously, public managers resisted programme evaluation because such processes demanded accountability for failures or shortfalls in goal achievements. Today, there is a much clearer understanding of performance measurement processes. From an internal perspective, identification of appropriate indicators should be specifically aligned with organizational goals and objectives. This way, performances measurement based on those indicators can offer in-depth programme assessments as well as guide the introduction and monitoring of corrective measures. From an external perspective, the selection of performance indicators needs to be appropriate to the shifting socioeconomic conditions of a country, while informed by both global and local circumstances.

Fourth, the quality and relevance of data collected on performance indicators can influence management effectiveness and performance evaluations of organizations and sectors. Programme and service quality can be enhanced by the consistency of well-designed data collection processes. The question of relevance—in other words what data to collect—may be answered in several ways because of differing categories of performance information. Decisions on the selection of appropriate indicators for performance measurement and the data to be collected may be guided by various factors such as the goals and objectives of the specific evaluation. In general, indicators of interest include resource expenditure, productivity as a result of internal activities and the impact of that productivity and the relationship between these. An additional and important indicator is demand, as it influences workload in public organizations and guides planning processes regarding resource allocation and operations.

Fifth, bottom-up citizen engagement encourages local ownership by providing feedback to governments on public policy implementation. Citizen engagement has additional functions and benefits for development such as giving citizens a voice in decision-making processes that affect their lives. Citizen engagement contributes to inclusive public planning processes in which the concerns of a greater number of the recipients of public goods and services can be examined and accommodated. Classical organizational theorists emphasize planning processes as a key objective in achieving organizational effectiveness. Planning maps the direction of an organization's activities. It supports efficient coordination processes and delegation of responsibility, thereby contributing to enhancing accountability. Therefore, local ownership of development objectives and some combination of horizontal and vertical engagement in planning, implementation and monitoring processes are important to achieving inclusive, responsive and accountable governance.

Sixth, this chapter, in its earlier pages, emphasized the key role of the State in development. The political system, as outlined in national constitutions, provides a framework for public participation and institutions for exercising civic rights in the development of a country. It provides stability by clarifying relative roles and responsibilities of major stakeholders, including not only the government at the national and local levels but also civil society, the private sector, donors and other major actors. Political competition can contribute to diversifying perspectives which, if resolved through inclusive processes, can contribute to the legitimacy of the political system.

Finally, Member States are encouraged to search for and document good local practices and learn to scale them up. This can reinforce the importance of human capital development, especially for country-specific challenges. Scaling up successful local practices can build capacity and contribute to strengthening governance and public administration.

In conclusion, to reform is to improve something that exists. To transform something changes its very nature to something else. For the State to transform the current development trajectory towards a more sustainable path, it must also transform current public governance towards greater responsiveness and accountability.

For transforming the current development trajectory towards a more sustainable path, current public governance needs transformation towards greater responsiveness and accountability.

The following chapters will analyse how governance can become more responsive and accountable at all levels to ensure that the new development agenda improves on the well-being of the people. ■

Chapter 2
Responsive governance

1. Responding efficiently and effectively to people's needs

Responsive public governance requires responding efficiently and effectively to people's real needs. This entails a resolve to anchor policies, strategies, programmes, activities and resources, taking into account people's expectations, with particular attention paid to local variations and ambitions.

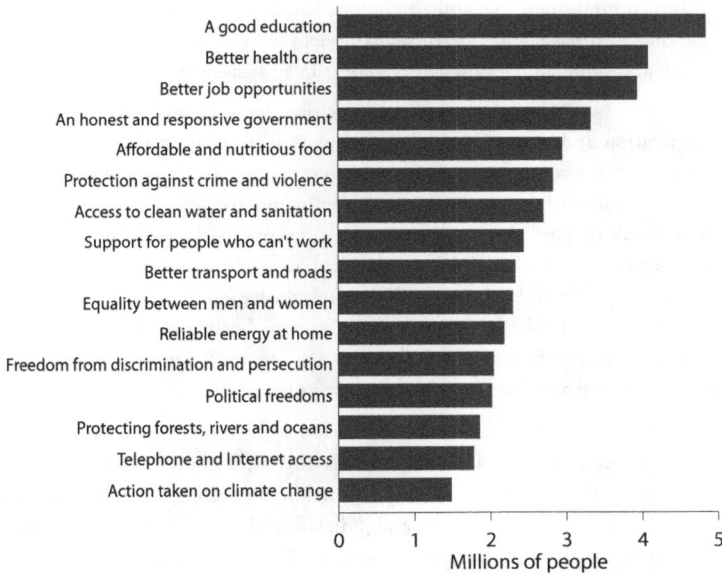

Horizontal bar chart titled "Millions of people" (x-axis from 0 to 5):

A good education	~4.8
Better health care	~4.1
Better job opportunities	~4.0
An honest and responsive government	~3.4
Affordable and nutritious food	~3.0
Protection against crime and violence	~2.9
Access to clean water and sanitation	~2.7
Support for people who can't work	~2.4
Better transport and roads	~2.3
Equality between men and women	~2.3
Reliable energy at home	~2.2
Freedom from discrimination and persecution	~2.0
Political freedoms	~2.0
Protecting forests, rivers and oceans	~1.9
Telephone and Internet access	~1.8
Action taken on climate change	~1.5

Source: United Nations (2015), My World. The United Nations Global Survey for a Better World. We the Peoples Celebrating 7 Million Voices.[52]

Responsive public governance requires a resolve to anchor policies, strategies, programmes, activities and resources on people's real needs.

As the deadline of 2015 for achieving the MDGs approaches, the world is still confronted with overwhelming challenges, despite significant gains. Based on CEPA report of April 2013, the United Nations Economic and Social Council underscored "the centrality of transparent, accountable, efficient, effective, non-discriminatory, professional and citizen-oriented public admin-

---

52 United Nations, modified image from "My World. The United Nations Global Survey for a Better World. We the Peoples Celebrating 7 Million Voices". Original image available from https://myworld2015.files.wordpress.com/2014/12/wethepeoples 7million.pdf.

istration … to the successful implementation of development policies and the management of development programmes …".[53]

To respond more efficiently and effectively to the multiple development challenges and identify people's real needs and aspirations, governments in many parts of the world have been collaborating with private businesses and civil society. Successfully undertaken, this collaboration enhances clarity and depth of understanding among parties and ultimately fosters more efficient and effective, and thus responsive, public policies. It also contributes to jointly prioritizing among the many competing needs to enhance the quality of life within communities. The United Nations has, in fact, recently acknowledged that the multi-stakeholder partnership model allows to "share burdens, catalyse action and bring all relevant actors to bear in addressing specific problems".[54]

The multi-stakeholder partner-ship model allows sharing burdens, catalysing action and bringing all relevant actors to bear in addressing specific problems.

Far beyond engagement through the electoral process, multisector cooperation and increased public participation in decision-making become a necessity for responsive action by governments. Addressing increasingly complex realities requires, in fact, a multidisciplinary approach and coherent policy-making while leveraging opportunities offered by collaboration with non-State actors. Such a multi-stakeholder partnership creates space for social entrepreneurship and innovation. When responsive governance is understood and practiced in this way, there can be burden-sharing and enhanced trust between the government and people. Citizens are no longer viewed passively as mere service recipients but also co-creators of public value.

Nevertheless, multisector cooperation adds complexities to traditional public governance and public institutions. The latter in many countries comprise, primarily, legislative bodies for rulemaking; specialized executive departments and their related agencies; and judiciaries which are responsible for rule interpretation, adjudication and dispute resolution. Modern administrations need to be able to respond to demand for participation in public affairs by setting up appropriate legal frameworks, designated organizational functions, and reliable channels and modalities. In addition to their ongoing service delivery, they need competency for promoting, regulating and managing collaboration among levels of government and different sectors. They need to be capable of implementing strategies that integrate social, economic and environmental aspects. All this ultimately is aimed at coordinating policy implementation

---

53 United Nations Committee of Experts on Public Administration, Report on the Twelfth Session, New York 15-19 April 2013 (E/2013/44-E/C.16/2013/6), p. 2. Available from www.unpan.org/DPADM/CEPA/12thSession/tabid/1544/language/en-US/Default.aspx.

54 United Nations, A life of dignity for all: accelerating progress towards the Millennium Development Goals and advancing the United Nations development agenda beyond 2015 (see A/68/202).

by multiple organizations that share responsibility for programme and service efficiency and effectiveness for development outcomes.

Clearly, numerous challenges are associated with enabling transformative shifts that ensure that all benefit from growth and globalization in an environmentally sustainable way. How can governments take part in responsive governance with the goal of bringing everyone forward?[55] The challenges to sustain responsive governance with these collaborative and participatory features become even more complex when there is a divergence of objectives, views and arrangements among concerned actors and organizations. Public administrations need to overcome the challenges that arise from the way this diversity can impact the behaviour of informal groups and individuals as well as the difficulty of integrating them into formal political processes.

Competent, diverse and ethical public servants under a credible leadership, engaged citizens and empowered communities, and multichannel service delivery with e-participation features can contribute to transforming public institutions to be more responsive. To succeed, these endeavours will need to take into account a major obstacle to responsive governance the co-existence between formal versus informal rules of human behaviour.

Responsive governance also requires contextual sensitivity to, among other things, cultural traditions, power bases and public opinion. Those seeking to ensure that effective governance is in place must address all these aspects and not mistake compliance with formal requirements as successful implementation.[56] The challenge is not only to have formal mechanisms in place, but also that they are adequate to attaining sustainable development goals. ◆

2. Meeting increasing public demands and addressing declining public trust

The Internet and social media are enabling massive generation and analyses of information and the ability to rapidly share knowledge and experience. Citizens and other non-State actors are increasing their demand for having a say in shaping public policies and better public services. For instance, the proliferation of international and regional treaties and agreements on all aspects

55   United Nations Chief Executive Board High-Level Committee on Programmes, Issues Paper by the Vice-Chair, 26th Session (CEB/2013/HLCP-XXVI/CRP.9), para. 13.

56   Margaret Saner, Contribution to World Public Sector Brief 2013.

of life is evidence of international consensus on pressing issues. These need implementation at the national and subnational levels.

The diversity and, at times, contradictory needs of the various social groups pose as a challenge for all governance actors. Recognizing that a one-size-fits-all solution will not respond to specific and particular circumstances, the United Nations Committee of Experts in Public Administration "reiterated the importance of considering country differences. Programmes and projects were very specific to countries and, in that regard, history, culture, political regime types and structures were all highly relevant".[57] This advice can also be applied at subnational and local levels.

A key aspect of responsive governance is for governments to recognize that one source of growing public demand is a rights-based approach to development. Among the key messages emerging from the consultation undertaken on governance, under the aegis of the United Nations Development Group (UNDG) are the notions that international human rights standards and principles must underpin development, that gender responsive and rights-based governance systems are central for implementing equality goals, that access to justice and effective justice administration are enablers for development and human rights, among others.[58]

Responsive governments need to recognize that one source of growing public demand is a rights-based approach to development.

Responding efficiently and effectively to people's real needs requires engaging the public to identify and articulate its needs. Article 21 of the Universal Declaration of Human Rights[59] enshrines people's right to take part in public governance: "1) Everyone has the right to take part in the government of his country, directly or through freely chosen representatives". This right was reiterated in the International Covenant on Civil and Political Rights,[60] Article 25: "Every citizen shall have the right and the opportunity, without any of the distinctions mentioned in article 2 and without unreasonable restrictions: (a) To take part in the conduct of public affairs, directly or through freely chosen representatives: ...". At the national level, the right to political and civic par-

---

57 Committee of Experts on Public Administration, Report on the 12th Session, New York 15-19 April 2013 (E/2013/44-E/C.16/2013/6), para. 55. Available from www.unpan.org/DPADM/CEPA/12thSession/tabid/1544/language/en-US/Default.aspx.

58 United Nations Development Programme, and Office of the High Commissioner of Human Rights, Global Thematic Consultation on Governance and the Post-2015 Development Framework: Consultation Report, September 2012 to March 2013, United Nations Development Project and United Nations Office of the High Commissioner of Human Rights.

59 United Nations, Universal Declaration of Human Rights, 1948 available on: http://www.ohchr.org/EN/UDHR/Documents/UDHR_Translations/eng.pdf.

60 United Nation, International Covenant of Civil and Political Rights, 1966 available at: http://treaties.un.org/doc/Publication/UNTS/Volume%20999/volume-999-I-14668-English.pdf.

ticipation is often guaranteed in the constitution. The United Nations Public Administration Country Studies, including a survey of the constitutions of all United Nations Member States, found that more than 150 countries enshrine the right of citizens to participate in one form or another.[61]

Because citizens are more likely to hold strong views on local matters that may affect their daily lives than on national issues, it may be easier for them to participate in decision-making at the local government level. Informal institutions, particularly those arising from culture and tradition or those used as social control mechanisms, will also be felt more keenly by individuals, particularly when stepping outside the accepted social norms could have repercussions on them personally or on their family. Because of this heightened relevance, the issue of context and consistency between the national and local, formal and the informal institutions becomes more important. Where the national versus local priorities and the formal and informal customs and practices are directly at odds, it would be very difficult if not impossible for a government to be responsive, unless measures are taken to reconcile the priority differences at the national and local levels and to alter the perceived value and impact of the formal and informal institutions.

The successful implementation of policies which have been adopted formally, for example through international treaty, but which run counter to local customs, must take into account the need to work with and usually change the power dynamic of the informal system. Examples include prevention of the transmission of HIV/AIDS, alternative rites of passage which obviate female genital mutilation or practices that are environmentally harmful. If communities are to be expected to give up their traditions, they must be persuaded of the benefits, with the aim of the majority choosing to change of their own accord. Otherwise, there is a risk that the informal traditions will simply be driven further underground. However, informal systems are not necessarily negative. They may assist, for instance, to address local concerns in underserved areas based on residents' voluntary contributions. The challenge is taking care not to diminish their benefits through imposed formal systems.[62]

When governance is perceived not to be responsive to people's needs, trust in government declines and may even threaten political and social stabil-

When governance is perceived not to be responsive to people's needs, distrust in government may be widespread and even threaten political and social stability.

---

61 United Nations Department of Economic and Social Affairs, the United Nations Public Administration Country Studies is internal research undertaken by the United Nations Department of Economic and Social Affairs, Division for Public Administration and Development Management, forthcoming. The constitutions of United Nations Member States were reviewed for keywords, serving as indicators of citizen engagement and freedom of information provisions.

62 Marie Byström, "Collective action and property rights (CAPRi)", Working Paper No. 31, in Formal and Informal Systems in Support of Farmer, Management of Agro-Biodiversity: Some Policy Challenges to Consolidate Lessons Learned (2004).

ity. Distrust results from a loss of confidence in administrative and political performance and dissatisfaction with public goods and services.[63] For half a century, public administration scholars have tackled the issue of trust in government. They have shown that when citizens believe that their governments are acting in their best interest, they are more likely to cooperate with public decision-makers. Such scholars have noted that perceptions of what is good may be vested in socially shared values and norms, which are likely to differ across national cultures.

This phenomenon is applicable also across organizational cultures. In partnering with diverse organizations, consensus on values and norms may be less achievable than within more organizationally homogenous arrangements. Access to public leaders and opportunities for interaction are necessary to facilitate communication and collaboration toward achieving consensus. Inclusive and public participation strategies are an integral aspect of building trust within and among organizations.

Public administration scholars observe that public trust is essential for maintaining the legitimacy and stability of political systems.[64] They also pointed out its economic and social benefits.[65] Trust in government encourages cooperation and compliance with laws and regulations, which are essential for good governance.[66] These observations advance the concept of a reciprocal relationship between public trust in governments and their associated organizations and responsive governance.

Public leaders in many parts of the world contemplated and undertook government reform to increase their efficiency in the face of increasing public needs and demands. While legislators make choices and decisions on behalf of the citizenry, the executive may both advise on and implement those decisions. There are variations around the world on this structure, but there is a general assumption that choices and decisions are made with the consent of citizens

---

63 Eric W. Welch, Charles C. Hinnat and M. Jae Moon, "Linking citizen satisfaction with e-government and trust in government". Journal of Public Administration Research and Theory, 15, (2004) pp. 371-391.

64 Caroline J. Tolbert and Karen Mossberger, "The effects of e-government on trust and confidence in government". Public Administration Review, 66 (2006), pp. 354-69.

65 Craig W. Thomas, "Maintaining and restoring public trust in government agencies and their employees". Administration and Society, 30, (1998) pp. 166-193.

66 Lan Ayres and John Braithwaite, Responsive Regulation: Transcending the Deregulation Debate, (New York: Oxford University Press 1992); Margaret Leviand Laura Stoker "Political trust and trust worthiness", Annual Review of Political Science, 3, (2000), pp. 475-507; John T. Scholz and Mark Lubell, "Trust and taxpaying: testing the heuristic approach to collective action", American Journal of Political Science, 42 (1998) pp. 398-417; Tom R. Tyler, Why People Obey the Law. (New Haven, CT: Yale University Press).

and in their best interest. Nationally, where there is democracy, there will be an established mechanism to elect or remove the legislators. In recent years, the world has seen what can happen when the citizenry chooses not to give its consent to the decision- makers. However, it must be borne in mind that a government may legitimately make choices or decisions that some citizens do not favour. It may be for the general good such as in cases when harmful substances are prohibited. Or it may be with the aim of benefiting the future economy such as in cases where some localities may feel they are disadvantaged when road building to support trade has a detrimental effect on local landowners.

Such choices and decisions are legitimized by the democratic context and by the process of analysing the options and of decision-making. Citizens may well be prepared to accept choices that do not benefit them personally if they believe that the process to arrive at that decision was fair and reasonable and beneficial overall. Conversely, if a policy is seen to be unfair, unworkable or unenforceable, it will not be embraced. The greater the trust and confidence in the decision-makers, the more likely the public is to accept unpalatable choices. In the past, it may have been the case that a paternalistic style of government could operate wherein legislators (and often the executive) took the attitude that they "knew best". But in the present information age, administrations have recognised that they must take into account the citizens' views. Engagement with citizens, both as recipients of services and as stakeholders in policy development and implementation, has become a priority and an integral part of responsive governance. ◆

Public policies are not embraced when citizens do not believe the process to arrive at these measures was fair, reasonable and beneficial overall.

3. Competent, diverse and ethical public servants

Public service is the connecting link between the state and the people. As such, it responds to public demands and is the incubator of public trust or mistrust in government.[67] Determinants of trust include technical and professional capacities, professionalism, ethics, integrity, transparency, accountability, effectiveness and responsiveness of public servants in conducting public affairs and delivering goods and services to the people.

Appropriate regulatory frameworks have to guide public servants and their leaders to behave in ways that meet public expectations. Civil service laws or codes, public service standing orders, codes of conduct and specialized

A focus on satisfying the people's expectations in terms of quality, quantity, equity and promptness of the services delivered is critical to enhanced responsiveness.

---

67 United Nations, World Public Sector Report 2001, "Globalization and the state" (ST/ESA/PAD/SER.26).

leadership codes are used in public service regimes the world over. These tend to focus more on the "inward" aspects of the public service, especially compliance with values, norms, rules, procedures, and even etiquette. Service standards, citizens' charters, and quality assurance programmes tend to focus more on the "outward" aspects, especially satisfaction of the expectations of recipients in terms of quality, quantity, equity and promptness of the services. These two types of frameworks complement one another and need to be adopted concurrently to enhance responsiveness and increase trust in government.[68]

In 2012, the Department of Economic and Social Affairs (DESA) of the United Nations, through its Division for Public Administration and Development Management (DPADM) researched "inward" aspects of public service values and standards of conduct in the 193[69] United Nations Member States. This was achieved through a review of their codes of ethics, codes of conduct, appropriate sections of national civil service laws, etc. aimed at creating the United Nations Public Administration Country Studies (UNPACS). According to the review, 62 Member States, or 61 per cent of those with codes, include professionalism in their behaviour codes as a desired value (see annex for additional information). There are variations in the type and detail of formal mechanisms for operationalizing this value, but the intention is to prevent poor performance and to provide predictability for both public servants and citizens, through creating and managing expectations.

Ideally, all organizations that collaborate in the delivery of public services should maintain standards of professionalism among their employees and with the public that they serve. Performance cannot be isolated from responsiveness to the needs of the citizenry. Nonetheless, only 30 Member States, or 30 per cent of those with codes, appears to include responsiveness among the most relevant standards of conduct in the public service (see annex for additional information).

Public servants must develop the requisite knowledge, skills and attitudes to consult and partner with stakeholders to effectively respond to their needs.

Public servants, including senior political and technical leaders, must develop the requisite competence of knowledge, skills and attitudes to consult with citizens and partner with a broad range of stakeholders to effectively respond to their needs. In meeting the challenges of the 2030 Agenda for Sustainable Development , public servants that are "trained to operate bureaucratic hierarchical systems ... have got not only to unlearn this but also to learn new ways of engaged and participatory administration".[70]

---

68 United Nations Committee of Experts on Public Administration, Report on the 7th Session, New York, 14-18 April 2008 (E/2008/44–E/C.16/2008/6).

69 UNPACS research shows that 101 Member States have formalized codes of conduct.

70 United Nations Committee of Experts on Public Administration, Report of the Seventh Session, New York, 14-18 April, 2008 (see E/2008/44–E/C.16/2008/6).

Public servants can contribute to responsive governance through developing new competencies which can help to tackle complex challenges—for instance, "systems thinking" for problem solving and "organizational development".[71] These competencies fundamentally change the way policy and services are developed, such as a "whole-of-government" approach. Actions are no longer seen and planned in a linear way but as complex interactions among elements of a system. The "system" may be internal or external to an organization. Recognizing and mapping these systems are the basis for improving or regulating them. "Analysis of systems in use will highlight where there are risks to the formal system, where informal systems are in place, and facilitate the assessment of the level of risk and the potential for redesign or contingency planning. In practice this must involve people from all elements of the system so that the true picture is built up and assumptions are not made which might lead to poor design".[72]

Organizational development theory and concepts also offer ways to understand power in systems, stakeholder expectations, and options for influencing behaviour. Government decisions are primarily about when and how to intervene, whether to regulate, incentivize or penalize. Understanding systems and human behaviour alongside economic and legal issues is essential to effective policy development. In some administrations, officials are subject matter experts while in others, they are drawn from economic or legal cadres. In order to secure replicable policies, expertise and evidence should be drawn from all relevant sectors, and citizens consulted to ensure that proposals are realistic. The current complexity of many issues to be addressed by governments requires a competency of collaboration among officials. Hence, a responsive public service is impartial and professional, drawing where appropriate on the skills and resources of the private and civil society sectors.[73]

A diverse public service can better interact and take into account public opinion, engage with citizens and be more responsive to their needs.

Besides developing requisite competency, the complexity also calls for a public service that is diverse and representative of the whole community it serves. A diverse public sector workforce—composed of women and men as well as members of all ethnic, religious and other social groups—increases the collective understanding of societal aspirations. It can also enhance rigorous policy development processes, based on consultation, evidence and problem-solving methodologies. In fragile states, a representative, merit-based service-

---

71 Peter M. Senge, The Fifth Discipline: The Art and Practice of the Learning Organization. Doubleday: revised and updated edition, 2006.

72 Margaret Saner, Contribution to World Public Sector Brief 2013.

73 World Public Sector Report 2005,"Unlocking the human potential for public sector performance" (see ST/ESA/PAD/SER.E/63).

oriented public service can serve as a model for participation, inclusive decision-making, reconciliation and social cohesion, and proactive peace building.[74]

Moreover, a diverse public service provides credible rationale for choices and decisions and moves administrations beyond short-term solutions, or those based on the preferences of a vocal minority. Box 2.1 (below) presents an example of responding to the needs of women and children through gender responsive budgeting.

Even with a competent and diverse public service, responsiveness will be diminished or subverted when public servants behave unethically or engage in -outright acts of corruption. Formal regulations can be circumvented by

Box 2.1: Morocco—Gender Responsive Budgeting (GRB)

Winner of 2014 UNPSA (Category: Promoting Gender-Responsive Delivery of Public Service)

Description: Incorporating a gender perspective in public policy, strategies and programmes and promoting equality and equity by integrating gender equality perspective into the budgets of ministries

Problem: Morocco faced challenges in promoting gender equality. A survey on the condition of women, launched in the Ministry of Economy and Finance (MEF), showed the untapped potential of women's expertise available in the Ministry. This raised the need for women to have a greater role in decision-making within the ministry. (Diversity within the public service, particularly at the decision-making level, can positively affect the understanding of needs and, hence, responsiveness to the community it serves.)

Solution: The Morocco-GRB programme is based on new instruments, including the institutionalized practice of submitting a gender report together with the draft budget law and budget guides. A feasibility study of the budgetary accounts of gender and children was conducted in 2002 in MEF, with the support of the World Bank, to produce appropriate instruments of GRB. MEF's application of GRB, with the partnership of UN Women, increased appropriation for key political stakeholders so as to transform financial governance. This transformation was achieved also through training budget planning officials of ministries, parliamentarians and selected NGOs. The Ministry called for applications by women to encourage their access to positions of responsibility. This process was accompanied by a fiscal reform. The latter acted as a catalyst for the integration of the gender equality into the budgets of ministries, leading to the implementation of the GRB in the country.

Impact: During 2013, a good practice Centre for Gender Responsive Budgeting was created within MEF. Also, the number of ministries that adhered to GRB was brought to 30, corresponding to almost 80 per cent of the total state budget. The gradual inclusion of the gender dimension in the planning and programming of ministries adopting GRB resulted in improved performance indicators for their policies and programmes.

Method used: Gender responsive budgeting through fiscal reform, surveys, gender reports, manuals and workshops

For more information: www.unpan.org/United Nations Public Service Awards.

---

[74] United Nations World Public Sector Report 2010, "Reconstructing public administration after conflict: challenges, practices and lessons learned" (ST/ESA/PAD/SER.E/135).

informal rules, operating for private benefit rather than the public good. Common examples are found in public procurement exercises when conflicts of interest can procure substandard goods and poor services and in recruitment and appointment procedures when candidates are chosen based on favouritism or political expediency rather than on merit. Other examples include lack of accountability for misconduct or poor performance. In the past, confidentiality had been invoked to shroud even egregious misconduct, particularly among senior officials. This situation is increasingly not sustainable in countries where civil society and the media have access to information and call for accountability. A public service that is ethical and seen to be ethical can greatly boost public and investor confidence.

Responsive governance requires public servants to act beyond orders and to be proactive. To strengthen responsiveness of the public service, capacity-building in areas such as innovation, customer and citizen focus, leading through influence, collaboration, project management, financial management and negotiation, among many others, will be required. Foremost, there is a need to inculcate a firm commitment to serving citizens.

Responsive governance and public administration call for an overhaul of the traditional public service both in its structure and human behaviour.

The improvement of quality, quantity and promptness of public goods and services calls for putting the citizen at the centre of public service delivery. However, institutions, systems, structures, processes and procedures of the public service often are not designed to support responsive delivery of goods and services. Thus, responsive governance and public administration calls for restructuring both the traditional public service and public servants' behaviour around people's needs.

As mentioned earlier, building trust between government and citizens is also necessary for promoting an open dialogue and both government-to-citizen (GtoC) and citizen-to-government (CtoG) exchange of information. Open communication ultimately helps governments to address the challenge of identifying and articulating the needs of the people. Against this backdrop, responsive governance becomes a complex, dynamic process, firmly rooted in the relevant contexts, whether national or local. ◆

4. Engaged citizens and empowered communities

Reaching out to and engaging people to identify and articulate their needs is a daunting challenge for governments, even when they enjoy the full trust of their citizens. First, it is easy to underestimate the radical change in public servants' behaviour necessary to engage with citizens. For some, citizen engagement may require courage; for others, it may mean an unfamiliar decision-making process, requiring additional time and resources. A cultural change in government and society is required to bring engagement to life, along with the human capital and skills necessary for meaningful participation. To this end, capacity and skills need to be developed within the public and private sectors as well as civil society. A sense of individual responsibility within the public service should be nurtured alongside the collective responsibility embodied in public governance institutions and processes.

Second, empowering communities includes outreach to the socially marginalized and vulnerable groups. A human rights-based development approach demands that all citizens—irrespective of sex, age, religion, ethnicity, origin, economic and social status—have the opportunity to participate in decision-making processes that affect their lives. In fact, the influence of citizens, especially the traditionally marginalized groups, on policymaking is critical for basic services to reach those who need them most. A dialogue between the government and the citizenry can lead to policies that have greater impact. Decentralized governance, in particular, is instrumental for fostering development which takes place at the local community level. Local governments can achieve better results by engaging local communities as they may be more in tune with local needs and may find local solutions to address them.

Box 2.2 (page 39) shows an example of institutional arrangement—the Inter-council Forums (IF)s and the national conferences preparatory discussions—adopted in Brazil since 2011 to foster participatory planning. At the same time, engagement allows achieving efficiency in addition to greater effectiveness as well as access to a wider range of resources. This is the case when civil society and the private sector join governments to coproduce public services.

Responsive governance is not about administering citizens but about collaborating with them in order to achieve common objectives.

Citizen engagement can occur at economic, political, social and cultural levels. It can also have different degrees, ranging from a one-way provision of information and consultation to two-way collaboration with citizens and involvement of them in decision-making and even oversight. According to the United Nations Committee of Experts on Public Administration, responsive governance is not about administering citizens but about collaborating with them in order to achieve common objectives.[75] To this end, governments must lead the way by creating opportunities for effective participation through

---

[75] United Nations, Report of 12th Session of the Committee of Experts on Public Administration, New York 14-18 April 2013, (E/2013/44–E/C.16/2013/6).

Box 2.2: Brazil—Inter-council Forum (IF)

Submission qualifying for 2012 UNPSA 2nd evaluation round (Category: Fostering Participation in Policy-making Decisions through Innovative Mechanisms)

Description: Strengthening social participation in local planning and budgeting processes backed by an integrated planning and budgeting information system

Problem: The difficulty in influencing the public agenda by the economically disadvantaged, migrant, or indigenous people, especially on issues of concern for minorities and vulnerable populations dissociated national planning; and the implementation of sectoral public policies. This negatively affected the design of a common agenda for national development. Since 1980s, various social organizations and movements began demanding the establishment of specific institutional channels to bring the voices of people into the planning and budgeting processes.

Solution: The President of Brazil set a goal to develop an institutional design that would meet the expectations of government and society. Participatory methodologies and channels that could influence national planning were established. The Inter-council Forums (IF)s and national conferences for preparatory discussions were held since 2011, which involved various civil society organizations, the general public and public officials. About 300 non-governmental representatives from more than 30 national councils and over 80 civil society organizations attended the 1st IF, in two days of meetings. The 2nd IF had 200 participants in Brasilia, with simultaneous videoconferencing sessions held in 6 other states, for a day. The 3rd IF was composed of 200 participants from over 30 councils and more than 60 civil society organizations in three days of meetings

Impact: In the first IF, more than 800 recommendations were received and synthesized into 600 proposals. There was a 97 per cent convergence (77 per cent complete and 20 per cent partial) between what was proposed by the society and what was later submitted to the National Congress as part of government planning. There was unprecedented long-term and large-scale transformation of the relationship between the government of Brazil and the Brazilians, both in the design of the participatory process and in the results.

Method used: Participatory meetings, conferences, public consultations, and public policy-design

For more information: www.unpan.org/United Nations Public Service Awards.

democratic institutions, civic education, information sharing and institutional responsiveness.[76]

The United Nations has been using a three-level model of citizen engagement that moves along a passive to active continuum.[77] The model includes: 1) information that enables participation by providing citizens with public information and access to information upon demand, 2) consultation by engaging citizens in deeper contributions to and deliberation on public policies and services and 3) decision-making by empowering citizens through co-design of policy options and co-production of service components and delivery

---

76   United Nations, video message from Ms. Haiyan Qian, former Director Division for Public Administration and Development Management, on the occasion of the Experts Group Meeting on Citizen Engagement in Post 2015 Development Agenda 3-4 December 2012, Beirut, Lebanon.

77   United Nations, E-Government Survey: E-Government for the Future We Want, ST/ESA/PAD/SER.E/188, 2014, p. 63, available from http://unpan3.un.org/egovkb/Portals/egovkb/Documents/un/2014-Survey/Chapter3.pdf.

modalities. This model of citizen engagement is based on the assumption that a shift from more passive to active engagement brings about true empowerment of people.

Third, meaningful engagement needs some prerequisites, including strong political commitment, access to information, an enabling environment in terms of comprehensive legal and institutional frameworks, structures and processes, complemented by capacity building. The first step entails the provision of public information. Public information can be manipulated into propaganda, but responding to citizens' requests for access to information is important for transparency and accountability.

Access to information or freedom of information usually begins in constitutions as a political or civic right. In 2012, UNPACS showed that provisions granting the right to information are contained in 118 or 62 per cent of the United Nations Member States' constitutions (see annex for additional information). Furthermore, 92 Member States have enabled these provisions through legislation or regulation on freedom of information or access to information. However, only 14 Member States, or 15 per cent, have freedom of information laws that specifically refer to the explicit purpose of engaging citizens (see annex for additional information).

Access to information is an essential preparatory step toward citizen engagement. It is also an indication of governments' commitment towards transparency.

Not only is access to information an essential preparatory step toward citizen engagement, but it is also an indication of governments' commitment towards transparency, which is another essential element for building trust. Of the countries providing for the right to information, 80 or 41.5 per cent of the 193 United Nations Member States institutionalize processes for providing access to public information (such as timeframes, charges for information-related services, languages, availability of appeal mechanisms when access is denied, etc.). These provisions are linked to obligations among public personnel to render services responsively and efficiently, within required timeframes.

Governments may be legally obligated to provide information in multiple languages and formats. Twelve per cent of the United Nations Member States, where freedom of information laws are in place, make these provisions (see annex for additional information). These are critical to giving access and inclusiveness and particularly important in countries with multilingual populations.

UNPACS also reviewed the policy and regulatory frameworks as well as the organizations established by Member States to consult with citizens or groups of citizens. In the economic and social spheres, the consultative institutions include, but are not limited to, economic and social councils (ESCs), councils of tripartite or multi-stakeholders, or national advisory councils on development. 65 countries or 34 per cent of UN membership have legal provisions enabling institutionalized public consultations and participation through an economic and social council or similar institution. The purpose and organizational arrangements of these institutions vary among Member States. ESC members can be appointed or elected by the legislature. There may be explicit requirements and arrangements for consultative processes, etc. (see annex for additional information).

Although many countries have well established and formalized mechanisms for citizens to come together, other consultative mechanisms remain informal. In general, the mere existence of formal provisions for engaging citizens does not offer a guarantee that Member States successfully implement them. Nor does it automatically translate into meaningful engagement of their citizens or empowered communities. Informal influences may in fact support or subvert legislation enforcement. "What is important is to make use of informal mechanisms as one of the means of engaging citizens rather than to attempt to formalize and possibly weaken, a useful conduit for consultation and implementation".[78]

Member States that successfully engage and consistently take into account needs expressed by various social groups are more likely to have responsive public policies and programmes. Box 2.3 (page 42) provides an example of empowering communities to plan, use public resources, and implement poverty reduction projects and strategies at the community level in Rwanda.

Member States that successfully engage and consistently take into account needs expressed by various social groups are more likely to have responsive public policies and programmes.

These, in turn, are more likely to be instrumental in enhancing social, economic and environmental development outcomes. Finally, the emphasis on citizen engagement has helped prevent or resolve some conflict and laid the foundations for a more peaceful society.[79] ◆

5. Multi-channel service delivery and e-participation

The explosion of digital connectivity, significant improvements in information and communication technologies (ICTs) paired with an ever increasing stakeholder engagement are revolutionizing the governance system and delivery of public services. Governments can deliver web-based and mobile services in addition to traditional ways, thus introducing multichannel service delivery.

---

78 Margaret Saner, Contribution to World Public Sector Brief 2013.

79 World Public Sector Report 2010, "Reconstructing public administration after conflict: challenges, practices and lessons learned" (ST/ESA/PAD/SER.E/135).

Box 2.3: **Rwanda—Ubudehe**

Winner of 2008 UNPSA (Category: Improving Transparency, Accountability and Responsiveness in the Public Service)

Description: Empowering citizens at the community level in Rwanda to plan, use public resources and implement poverty-reduction projects and strategies.

Problem: After the 1994 Rwanda genocide, the government inherited a country marked by poverty, inequality, trauma, fear and political and social apathy. The government faced the challenge of rebuilding a nation, including its public administration, infrastructure and basic services. The Ubudehe initiative sought to address three key challenges: 1) reducing citizen apathy towards government and towards their own problems, 2) building trust among the citizens so as to work together and build social capital and increased inclusiveness and 3) influencing and informing national decision makers with data generated by citizens.

Solution: This traditional mutual assistance and people-centered initiative, called Ubudehe, emerged thanks to the vision and active engagement of several key stakeholders from the Rwandan Government and also from the local government. The aim is to demonstrate the power of citizen participation in its truest form by bringing community members together to assess their socioeconomic conditions, exercise their own power to analyse, define their priorities and needs, and decide on what to do in order to improve their well-being by mapping out solutions for their problems. The Ubudehe enabled village residents to increase their own problem-solving capabilities and encouraged them to rely on their own ideas. Besides, it empowered decentralized administrative entities by financing development projects. The resources were disbursed directly from a donor to the Central Bank to citizens in the villages with no intermediary.

Impact: Ubudehe scaled up from 600 cellules, the smallest administrative area in Rwanda, to more than 9,154 cellules throughout the nation. Over 10,000 village actions emerged. Over 17,500 cascade facilitators were trained by the master trainers of the Ministry of Local Government. The initiative influenced the production of information, social maps, performance measures and national statistics about poverty, developing financial systems to transfer funds directly to citizens' accounts at the local level. In 2006-2007, across 9,000 villages, citizens came together to solve the problems they had highlighted.

Method used: Problem solving, participatory planning and budgeting through direct engagement, social capital building through strong partnership, capacity for monitoring accountability and transparency actions

For more information: www.unpan.org/United Nations Public Service Awards.

The enormous potential of ICT tools for greater efficiency, cost reduction, quality of public services, convenience, innovation and learning are being explored by governments around the world. ICT provides means to improve the quality and responsiveness of public services, expand the reach and accessibility of both services and public infrastructure, and allow citizens to experience faster and more transparent forms of access to government services.

Building enterprise architectures and integrated systems have enabled multi-channel provision of services. In addition, such an approach has allowed for the establishment of different forms of public service delivery from "one stop shop" for basic public service delivery to the "whole of government" approaches where each and every service involves multiple agencies. It has also increasingly centralized the entry point of service delivery to a single portal where citizens can access all government-supplied services, regardless of which government authority provides that service. Examples of benefits of online and mobile-based services include avoiding long commutes to public offices, accessing multiple services through single online windows, or even the possibility of accessing services outside regular office hours. It is important that online delivery is well-integrated into traditional offline methods, which still constitute the preferred modalities.

ICT also helps governments to share information with citizens and is becoming an effective measure to enhance their e-participation in decisions about policies and service delivery options. By combining traditional public administration concepts with new technologies, governments have increasingly been able to reach out to citizens on a previously unmatched scale. Broadband and mobile technology advances can and have promoted digital participatory decision-making methods. Box 2.4 (page 44) demonstrates how continuous dialogue with interested stakeholders can be maintained.

An open and honest dialogue with citizens, whether online or face-to-face, can lead to better government policies and services.[80] Some governments have been actively promoting e-participation, using the Internet or mobile technology to engage a much wider range of stakeholders in public policy-making. Social media, e-surveys, e-focus groups, e-citizen assemblies and e-networks can increase public participation and citizen engagement in shaping effective responses to their needs. "Such consultative mechanisms will be integral to governance systems of the future, and there is much to learn from the experiences of countries that have been active in this field".[81] Moreover, recent developments in many parts of the world have unequivocally shown that ignoring public opinion is a risk to public trust.

Social media, e-surveys, e-focus groups, e-citizen assemblies and e-networks can increase public participation and citizen engagement in shaping effective responses to their needs.

Multichannel service delivery and e-participation are part of e-government. E-government can bring about a number of benefits if implementation is well coordinated, managed and resourced, leading to 1) improved government administrative efficiency, effectiveness and productivity as well as information provision and service delivery to the public; 2) reduced administrative, operational and transactional costs of governments' administrative activities, service delivery functions and operations by reducing operational inefficiencies, redundant spending and unnecessary excessive paperwork; 3) improved ways and means in which governments serve citizens and businesses enhancing gov-

---

80 United Nations, see E/2009/44 E/C.16/2009/5. 09-31502 11.

81 United Nations, Video Message from Ms. Haiyan Qian, former Director, Division for Public Administration and Development Management, on the occasion of the Capacity Development Workshop on Citizen Engagement and the Post-2015 Development Agenda held in Beirut, Lebanon, from 5-6 December, http://www.youtube.com/watch?v=D1Pynb3cfDA.

Box 2.4: Moldova—Increased transparency in the decision-making process

1st Place Winner of 2013 UNPSA (Category: Fostering Participation in Public Policy Decision Making through Innovative Mechanisms, Europe and North America)
Description: Increasing transparency in decision-making processes and effectiveness of public policies.

Problem: A lack of strategic partnership between government, civil society and private sector. One of the main reasons for not promoting active citizen participation was the lack of guidelines in elaborating a public policy. Each ministry had a distinct approach to solving a specific issue, which usually did not take into the account the impact of the decision on different social groups which were affected by the public policy.

Solution: 24 websites of ministries and central public authorities were connected through one web portal to streamline the process of public consultations and to reduce the number of websites people needed to visit to find out what were the government's next steps in terms of public policies. The State Chancellery introduced the "participation module", which is the technical solution for organizing public consultations online. Everyone can now comment on everything that was posted online. The National Council for Participation was created, consisting of 30 representatives of civil society, in order to increase the participation of civil society in all government activities and to institutionalize continuous dialogue.

Impact: The government delivered a one stop solution to all citizens who gave them the permission to comment and to evaluate all public policies, developed by the government, and to participate in the decision making process. The traffic increased from 2,000 unique visitors at the launch of the site to over 18,000. All information regarding public consultation and public participation is streamlined.

Method used: Continuous dialogue with stakeholders, training of public servants and citizens, development of policy in the area of decision-making, transparency, streamlining IT solutions

For more information: www.unpan.org/United Nations Public Service Awards.

ernment's responsiveness to their needs; 4) transformed government systems through a citizen-centered focus and facilitating the process of bringing the government closer to the people; and 5) improved access to information and government services by the public.

The potential of e-government in developing and least developed countries, however, is still not fully exploited. The required human, organizational and technological resources remain challenges for many developing countries. However, e-government is a multidimensional and complex issue, which requires a broad definition and understanding for designing and implementing a successful e-strategy. The adoptive challenge of e-government goes far beyond technology; it calls for organizational structures and skills, new forms of leadership, transformative public and private partnerships, a new degree of civic participation, and so on.

E-government increases cooperative relations within governments and between the public sector, citizens and business users to enhance government responsiveness.

As a key factor for e-government development, an e-government strategy encompasses a country's vision on the use of ICT in government, the level of leadership commitment as well as the institutional framework required for its implementation. It is a key priority for governments to ensure that their policies, including the e-government strategy, are integrated, coherent and responsive to multidimensional and interconnected challenges and needs. 131

Member States have, therefore, prepared and adopted e-government strategies, spanning from a few years to 20 years. In Europe, the percentage of Member States having a national e-government strategy is the highest (79 per cent), followed by Oceania, Africa, Asia and the Americas (see annex for additional information).[82]

According to CEPA, "technology and e-government are enablers of more efficient, transparent, participatory and accountable governance".[83] The adoption of an e-government strategy requires going far beyond technology issues. It calls for new forms of service delivery, leadership, transformative public and private partnerships, and participatory processes among other outcomes. Opportunities provided by strategies on the use of ICT to improve government responsiveness include: 1) cost reduction and efficiency gains, 2) enhanced quality of public services delivered to business and customers, 3) networking and community creation, 4) improvement of the quality of decision-making, and 5) promotion of the use of ICT in other sectors of society. ◆

6. Lessons learned

As presented at the beginning of this chapter, people around the world have included honest and responsive government among their top priorities. In the face of this public expectation, governance needs to become more responsive to overcome the daunting, interconnected and increasingly complex challenges to attain sustainable development for all. Focusing on satisfying people's expectations in terms of quality, quantity and promptness of the public services delivered within the limited resources available is becoming more important to enhance public sector responsiveness.

Responsive governance requires all actors, led by governments, to be sensitive to a rights-based approach to development when the needs of citizens may vary widely. Being responsive to increasing public demand for services and how they are delivered requires governments, with their partners, to consider

---

82 United Nations Public Administration Country Studies (UNPACS), gather information on the national and sectorial e-government strategies, as well as legal and institutional frameworks at the national level. See annex for more information.

83 United Nations, Report on the 13th Session of the Committee of Experts on Public Administration, New York, 7-11 April, 2014 (see E/2014/44-E/C.16/2014/6). Available from http://workspace.unpan.org/sites/Internet/Documents/UNPAN92994.pdf.

equality and equity in the provision of goods and services as well as access to them.

Responsiveness is linked to trust in government, which in turn, is essential for encouraging cooperation and compliance with laws and regulations. There is therefore a reciprocal relationship between public trust in governments and their associated organizations, and responsive governance.

Experience points to responsive governance being hinged on a resolve to anchor policies, strategies, programmes, activities and resources on people's real needs. The latter must be fully understood and addressed by coherent policies and strategies that leave "no one behind". To do so, a competent, diverse and ethical public service is needed. Public servants must engage with citizens and strive to help communities to be empowered to articulate both their problems and possible solutions. Member States that successfully engage and consistently take into account needs expressed by various social groups are more likely to have responsive public policies and programmes.

Traditional delivery modalities such as face-to-face services, letters, telephones, faxes, integrated kiosks, among others, may continue to be preferred modalities by citizens. However, new measures that harness the outreach power of ICT can be integrated with the traditional ones to provide multichannel service delivery. All governance actors can tap into technical and social innovations, such as e-participation, for meeting the challenges of sustainable development.

While providing opportunities for increasing responsiveness, e-government strategies face challenges in their implementation. The 2014 United Nations e-Government Survey has identified and grouped such challenges in six dimensions of today's e-government: 1) implementing the whole-of-government approach; 2) adopting multichannel service delivery; 3) fostering e-participation; 4) addressing the digital divide that affects vulnerable groups; 5) enhancing usage; and 6) promoting openness of government data. These are the daunting challenges that developed and developing countries face in achieving progress towards providing better public services to their citizens and building a more sustainable future by leveraging ICT in an innovative way.

More importantly, traditional governance and public administration systems rely on formal institutions, laws, rules, regulations procedures and processes. But governance practices, particularly in developing countries, exist also in informal systems which work alongside the formal ones.

Informal systems may have their own forms of discipline and convention affecting the behaviour of individuals or groups. Some of them may not be so clearly self-regulated and may subvert or challenge formal systems or simply provide a "parallel world" in which the formal rules are espoused but not adhered to and are, therefore, rendered impotent. As mentioned previously, the existence of informal institutions can impede formal health policy objectives such as the prevention of transmission of HIV/AIDS to subverting formal public procurement procedures. The formality or informality of systems is not relevant; what is important is how the needs of the people are identified, taken into account and responded to. Formal systems necessarily operate with an explicit objective and a clear and legal definition, while informal systems can be less explicit.

Attaining coherence between formal and informal organizations within society may be helpful. Separately, countries and organizations have made progress in identifying and engaging with informal systems; however, there are challenges. For example, in places where historically a command model of government has been sufficient to ensure compliance, citizens' expectations of a more participatory style of government expose the gap in the implementation process. When orders are immediately complied with, there is no need for consultation and agreement to proceed. A part of increasing the capacity of public servants may include raising their awareness of informal community structures that require consultation in order to successfully run development programmes for poverty eradication and empowering communities.

The information age and other social, (including demographic) factors, have fundamentally changed the relationship between citizens and the State. Due to geographic, cultural and historic variations, informal systems must be understood in the local context and the potential or the probability of them impacting the identification, discussion, consideration and response to the development needs assessed in each case. The onus is on policy developers to broaden their own appreciation of informal systems that might affect their advice. Mapping the types and themes of the more recognizable informal systems assists those engaged in policy implementation. In parallel, learning and development for those engaged in implementation will facilitate success in navigating what can be confusing and uncertain territory in relation to how the public will respond to proposals. Much is already known; it needs to be gathered together, focused and, most importantly, put into practice.

Governance is under the spotlight and, in accordance with their own requirements, administrations need to address capacity deficits in order to avoid problems and enhance their performance and responsiveness. This hinges on multisector trust, cooperation and increased public participation in decision-making as a critical component of transformative capacity needed to attain sustainable development. ■

Chapter 3
Accountable governance

1. Accountability for leveraging few and safeguarding new resources

The United Nation Secretary General has emphasized that: "Effective governance for sustainable development demands that public institutions in all countries and at all levels be inclusive, participatory and accountable to the people". [84]

Accountability takes many forms. They include political, managerial, fiscal, legal, and other dimensions. This chapter will focus on public accountability, which depends on transparency, or the "unfettered access by the public to timely and reliable information on decisions and performance in the public sector". [85] As such, it has two dimensions. One refers to having to provide information about one's actions (answerability). The other dimension refers to having to face consequences from those dissatisfied either with the actions themselves or with the rationale invoked to justify them.

Accountability is really about calling and holding institutions and officials to account in undertaking their functions or duties.

Accountability is really about calling and holding institutions and officials to account in undertaking their functions or duties. [86] Increasingly, the consequences for performance are also being invoked. In this sense accountable governance is linked to responsive governance.

Accountability can also be analysed from the perspectives of who is accountable, to whom, for what and how. Given the level of resources required, however, financial and performance accountability are priorities for the 2030 Agenda for Sustainable Development.

Financial accountability requires that public funds are used for the purpose for which they were intended. Accountability helps to ensure that public officials exercise their authority in a way that respects the law and is consistent with public sector values of economy, probity and stewardship. By safeguarding appropriate use of revenues raised from taxpayers, it also enhances public trust in government. This is particularly important within the context of implementing sustainable development initiatives.

By safeguarding appropriate use of revenues raised from taxpayers, accountability enhances public trust in government.

---

84 United Nations General Assembly, "The road to dignity by 2030: ending poverty, transforming all lives and protecting the planet", synthesis report of the Secretary-General on the post-2015 sustainable development agenda, A/69/700, 2014, para. 77, p. 19.

85 Integrity, transparency and accountability in public administration: recent trends, regional and international developments and emerging issues. Available from http://unpan1.un.org/intradoc/groups/public/documents/un/unpan020955.pdf.

86 Richard Mulgan, Holding Power to Account: Accountability in Modern Democracies, Palgrave Macmillan, 2003.

Accountability for performance facilitates checks and balances from internal and external stakeholders and serves to guide, monitor and evaluate public institutions and programmes as well as inform improvements. Hence, accountability denotes responsibility for results and outcomes. When operating effectively, it serves to ensure that public governance can flourish, related institutions can perform well and services are delivered to citizens effectively and efficiently.

Financial accountability has a critical role in safeguarding resources and ensuring that they are appropriately utilized for attaining sustainable development goals. In the Rio+20 conference's outcome document, the Member States recognized "the need for significant mobilization of resources from a variety of sources and the effective use of financing, in order to promote sustainable development".[87] Important for many low-income countries, official development assistance (ODA) reached $134.8 billion in 2011.[88] However not only the amount of aid but also its effectiveness, transparency and accountability need to be increased.

The Inter-governmental Committee of Experts on Sustainable Development Financing observed in its report: "Generally accepted principles of good budgeting address the stages of formulation, approval, execution and audit. These principles should ensure that public spending is consistent with national sustainable development strategies, inclusive of environmental, social, economic, gender and other goals. Planning and execution of budgets should be based on transparency, legitimacy, accountability and participation of citizens, consistent with country capabilities and circumstances. In this regard, domestic public sector internal and external control mechanisms, such as supreme audit institutions, which ensure that spending is in line with intended purposes should be implemented and strengthened. Furthermore, fiscal decentralization can strengthen local governance and create local ownership for the disposition of funds".[89]

Moreover, given the continuing impact of the global financial and economic crisis, ODA is increasingly being overtaken by other sources, streams and mechanisms of financing to meet the development needs forecasted beyond 2015.

The emergence of new aid providers and partnership approaches, which provide opportunities for aid to leverage private resource flows, determine changes in the aid architecture.[90] Despite their expression of political will in

---

87 United Nations, The Future We Want (A/CONF.216/1.1), 2012, para. 252.

88 United Nations, The Millennium Development Goals Report 2014, p. 48.

89 United Nation, Report of the Intergovernmental Committee of Experts on Sustainable Development Financing (A/69/315), 2014, para. 70.

90 United Nations, The Future We Want (see A/CONF.216/1.1), para. 260.

Rio, governments—already constrained in public spending—have to build trust in order to persuade potential new funders that their contributions will indeed be economically, efficiently and effectively dedicated to sustainable development initiatives. It is in their interest to demonstrate that the implementing agents of these initiatives—public administrations and their array of traditional and new partners—are focusing on "democratic governance, improved transparency and accountability, and managing for results".[91]

Traditional public administration measures, including planning, programme delivery, monitoring, evaluation and internal and external financial control, will need to be carried out in multiple jurisdictions under overlapping governance structures and rules, while satisfying a larger array of actors. Hence, it is not surprising that "... accountable and inclusive institutions at all levels" represent one of the SDGs.[92] This reinforces the earlier call for democratic governance and accountable institutions in the Millennium Declaration.

When public officials who implement a government's agenda are held to account by government representatives, they operate under a concept of hierarchical accountability.[93] A similar traditional model of accountability is one in which the line of authority operates upward, as well as downward, which is also called vertical accountability. For instance, a senior government official is held to account by a government minister, but that senior government official also holds other subordinate officials to account.

Accountability is really about calling and holding institutions and officials to account, in undertaking their functions or duties.

This type of accountability is internal to government and is described as "... a vertical chain that provides a continuum of accountability relationships between the electorate, Parliament, government, and the public service".[94] External to executive government are formal mechanisms such as supreme audit institutions, ombudsmen and other organizations that exist to ensure that accountability arrangements are met.

There are two types of accountability that reflect the modern reality, in the context of multiple public service delivery systems and their diverse accountability arrangements. They are shared accountability and social accountability. As accountability typologies, these transcend traditional hierarchical and vertical arrangements. Accountability is further discussed in this chapter with due consideration given to the role of professionalism in formal

---

91 Ibid., para. 258.

92 United Nations, Outcome Document of the Open Working Group for Sustainable Development Goals, Sustainable Development Knowledge Platform: Goal 16 http://sustainabledevelopment.un.org/focussdgs.html.

93 Meredith Edwards, Shared accountability in service delivery: concepts, principles and the Australian experience, Vienna Meeting July 2011.

94 Australian Public Service Commission, Delivering Performance and Accountability, Contemporary Government Challenges series, Commonwealth of Australia, (2009a).

institutions, the influence of informal governance institutions and the beneficial role of information and communication technology. ◆

2. Enhancing accountability to fight waste, mismanagement and corruption

In Rio in 2012, the Member States stressed that "fighting corruption and illicit financial flows at both the national and international levels is a priority and that corruption is a serious barrier to effective resource mobilization and allocation and diverts resources away from activities that are vital for poverty eradication, the fight against hunger and sustainable development".[95] "Illicit financial flows (due to crime, corruption, tax evasion and illicit activity) have become a matter of major concern because of the scale and systematic adverse impact of such flows on global governance and the development agenda. ... One estimate of untaxed off-shore wealth holdings puts the amount between $21 trillion and $32 trillion on the high end. ... On the low end, other studies estimated off-shore wealth holdings between $5.9 trillion and $8.5 trillion in different years".[96] Regional and global anti-bribery measures target the supply side of corruption.

A number of developing countries and countries with transitioning economies have significantly advanced on their targets towards the MDGs, despite the prolonged global economic downturn and resource shortages. In others, progress has been made in some key areas, for example, poverty reduction, improved access to education and health care. Nonetheless, performance has fallen below expectations in several other important areas, outside the MDG purview, such as building capacities for transparency and accountability in the delivery of public services. This lagging progress has made it difficult to prevent waste, avoid mismanagement and reduce corruption that continues to be widespread where the rule of law is not consistently respected and enforced. Whether viewed as a cause or consequence of underdevelopment, corruption diverts scarce public resources for private gain and distorts the distribution of public goods and services. In a context where the rule of law is not properly enforced, corruption destroys public trust in government. This may have

---

95 The Future We Want (see A/CONF.216/1.1), para. 266.

96 United Nations, World Economic Situation and Prospects 2015, p. 83, available from: http://www.un.org/en/development/desa/policy/wesp/wesp_archive/2015wesp_full_en.pdf.

a negative impact on financial investments and investors' confidence, which in turn—in combination with other microeconomic and general governance weaknesses—can have negative effects on economic development and inclusive equitable growth. Given the high and varied cost of fighting corruption, prevention through measures within and outside of the public sector is key to safeguarding resources.

The United Nations Convention against Corruption, which was ratified in 2005, recognized the importance of prevention by dedicating a chapter to various administrative practices and social measures. This Convention is the first legally binding global instrument for fighting corruption.

To reduce waste, mismanagement and corruption, governments need to prioritize sectors and public services where increasing transparency and accountability is critical. Specifically, accountability mechanisms and processes need to be strengthened in high-risk areas that involve large financial flows and are prone to corruption. These include public procurement, public works, concessions involving extractive industries and privatizations, among others. Informal practices prone to corruption and the value system within a society are key areas to be analysed. Box 3.1 (page 56) shows the example of the government of the Republic of Korea where measuring and publicizing integrity levels and corruption-prone tasks of public organizations has led to a decrease in corruption.

Establish and integrate stronger accountability, anticorruption and regulatory frameworks are essential to achieving the SDGs.

As a cornerstone of governance, accountability of public administrations is a prerequisite to and underpins public trust.[97] Public accountability is hampered by many challenges. In particular, challenges in developing countries can be considered in two groups: those relating to formal versus informal institutions of accountability, and those relating to shared responsibility where different public—and often private—actors deliver services.

Improving accountability in governance and public administration as a formal goal is extremely difficult in countries where informal arrangements frequently conflict with and supplement formal ones. Reform measures may target formal governance arrangements without acknowledging the implications of the informal structures in which many formal governance transactions take place. Ignoring these interactions means ignoring the difficulties in enforcing certain formal rules in a particular context. This also translates into a missed opportunity for designing formal rules with a better chance of achieving sustained development improvements.

---

97 Integrity, transparency and accountability in public administration: recent trends, regional and international developments and emerging issues, August 2005, United Nations Department for Economic and Social Affairs. Available from http://unpan1. un.org/intradoc/groups/public/documents/un/unpan020955.pdf.

The existence of informal rules and processes that support patron-client politics or political corruption is generally identified as a failure in governance.

Informal institutions may also have forms of enforcement, but the enforcement does not involve enforcement by formal state agencies. Powerful but informally organized special interest groups in society drive behaviour. The politics of patronage, the exchange of favours within informal networks and the use of informal resources to collaborate, construct and maintain political parties and other organizations fall into this category.

Box 3.1:   Republic of Korea—Integrity Assessment, Department of Public Administration

1ST Place Winners of 2012 UNPSA (Category: Preventing and Combating Corruption in the Public Service, Region: Asia and the Pacific)

Description: Assessing the integrity levels and corruption-prone tasks of public organizations

Problem: According to the Corruption Perceptions Index (CPI) released by Transparency International in 2000, the Republic of Korea ranked 48th among 90 countries, and a survey conducted by the Korea Independent Commission Against Corruption (KICAC) in 2002 showed that 48.1 per cent of Korean people believed that civil servants were corrupt.

Solution: The integrity assessment is designed to assess the corruption status of individual organizations and their specific tasks, rather than macro areas of public service. Only first-hand service users and internal staff of public organizations are surveyed about their corruption experience and perception, while the perception of the general public which might be inaccurate is excluded from the assessment.

Impact: Since the assessment officially started in 2002, the overall integrity index of the Korean public sector has increased consistently from 6.43 in 2002 to 8.43 in 2011. It seems that corruption experienced by citizens dealing with public service also has decreased substantially.

Method used: The assessment results point out the areas where corruption is the most severe so that each public organization can focus its efforts on addressing corruption in those specific tasks and improving relevant legal and institutional frameworks. The scores calculated from these results are disclosed to the public through the media, showing the integrity level of each public organization.

For more information: www.unpan.org/ United Nations Public Service Awards.

There may be informal enforcement of the "rules" by these organizations, according to partisan rather than public interests. They may also exclude those who do not accept particular informal rules from networks of influence and resource allocation. The latter can be a very credible enforcement mechanism, where life can be difficult for individuals outside these networks, particularly as is the case in many developing and transitioning countries.

The existence of informal rules and processes is generally identified as a failure in governance. In such contexts, patron-client politics or other forms of political corruption challenge accountability. Patron-client politics and the distribution of informal resources to powerful organizations are often the only viable strategy of maintaining political stability in contexts where many power-ful groups and organizations have no productive employment opportunities.[98]

The emergence of accountable governance, which is essentially govern-ance through effectively enforced formal rules, is a gradual process. It becomes viable when the most powerful organizations and groups accept the rule of law. Without the rule of law, the informal interpretation and selective enforcement of formal rules is a major problem for achieving broad-based developmental outcomes.

The emergence of accountable governance, which is essentially governance through effectively enforced formal rules, is a gradual process.

When much of the economy is either informal or dependent on one or two natural resources, the incentive to enforce formal institutions is not suf-ficiently broad-based. The state may not even have the resources to finance the effective enforcement of all formal institutions. Without a diversified economy and many productive formal organizations that pay significant taxes, there may not be the demand or the resources for the enforcement of formal institutions for sustaining productivity and competitiveness.

When the political system is accountable to many constituencies that are not yet committed to the rule of law, accountable governance will not be achieved only by reforming public administration or introducing new tools of accountability. Significant broad-based political and societal changes, includ-ing appropriate incentives in the informal sector, have to be found for govern-ance improvements.

Where there is greater state capacity, additional layers of complexity in accountability arrangements occur, for example, when more than one agency or more than one level of government agrees to share responsibility for out-comes. This type of accountability is often horizontal, therefore functional, where one government entity is not the only entity involved in delivering goods and services to the public.

Three types of arrangement are often observed: 1) responsibility for outcomes shared between two or more government agencies and their respec-tive ministers (e.g., to achieve a reduction in child poverty through health education); 2) between two or more levels of government with shared objec-tives (e.g., housing and agricultural services); and 3) between governments and non-government parties (e.g., private sector or not-for-profit organizations) that collaborate to deliver services to citizens (e.g. prisons or youth services).[99]

---

98 Mushtaq Husain Khan, "Markets, states and democracy: patron-client networks and the case for democracy in developing countries", Democratization 12 (5) 2005, pp. 705-725; Douglass C. North, John J. Wallis, Steven B. Webb and Barry R. Weingast (eds). In the Shadow of Violence: Politics, Economics and the Problems of Develop-ment. Cambridge: Cambridge University Press, 2013.

99 John Alford and Janine O'Flynn, "Rethinking public service delivery", Palgrave Mac-millan, 2012.

Additional layers of complexity in accountability arrangements occur when there is more than one agency or level of government agreeing to share responsibility of outcomes.

This last type of horizontal accountability, involving parties outside of government, is increasingly observed in service delivery arrangements. In turn, it can be divided into two types: a clearly identifiable formal transactional relationship, based on contract between the principal and agent; and collaborative, partnership or network relationships. This latter case is especially likely to be observed where both public and private agencies are together involved in achieving longer term outcomes and where there may not be a clearly defined principal or agent. The most common arrangement would be for shared decision-making as well as shared service delivery, including co-producing with communities or clients. A less common arrangement would be where the decision-making role is shared but the non-governmental partner delivers services.

Ensuring accountability in more collaborative or partnering arrangements of this kind presents challenges. Even if there is a mutual accountability established between the provider and government, it is often not clear who is ultimately responsible to the citizens. An extreme position is of those countries where aged care services, where services are delivered to citizens through profit-making and non-profit organizations, without any government presence at all. The question then is that if anything goes wrong, who is in charge, who is responsible, and to whom?

Despite implementation difficulties, finding effective mechanisms for sharing accountabilities offers promising opportunities. The Report of the United Nations Secretary-General on the Sixty-eighth Session of the General Assembly, in fact, highlights the importance of "a participatory monitoring framework for tracking progress and mutual accountability mechanisms for all stakeholders". [100]

In preventing waste, mismanagement and corruption, it is important to identify incentives for coherence of enforcement by formal and informal institutions as well as to clearly define and agree upon a framework of accountabilities among all organizations involved. ◆

---

[100] "A life of dignity for all: accelerating progress towards the Millennium Development Goals and advancing the United Nations development agenda beyond 2015 "Report of the Secretary-General from the Sixty-eighth Session of the General Assembly (see A/68/202). Available from www.un.org/millenniumgoals/pdf/A%20Life%20of%20Dignity%20for%20All.pdf.

3. Accountable public servants and public institutions for transparency

In addition to the formal and informal nature and sharing of account-abilities, the United Nations Committee of Experts on Public Administration recognizes that a "lack of professionalism and corruption in the public service are often institutional problems at their roots".[101] It is critical that institutional arrangements, structures, systems and practices of public organizations should be well functioning and performing. They should also be conducive to civic engagement, transparency and accountability for both exercising the power and the use of public funds entrusted to them by society.

With a view to guiding professional behaviour and preventing mis-conduct, criminality and abuse of power, many governments and public sec-tor organizations have adopted legislation or codes of conduct which set out the standards of behaviour expected and the penalties for failing to comply. Chapter 2 has already analysed the interaction between trust in government and a rule and value-based professional, efficient, effective, transparent, ethi-cal, accountable and responsive public service. However, when the behaviour of public servants contradicts these parameters, there is a lowering of trust in government. Almost all countries have legal or administrative provisions for guiding the behaviour of public servants. However, the actual conduct of pub-lic servants and negative public perceptions of their conduct in many countries illustrate in a practical way the challenges of accountable governance.

Public institutions responsible for the protection of citizens' rights to government information further enhance accountable governance. These rights can be enshrined in the constitution and promulgated through Freedom of Information (FOI) laws. As mentioned in Chapter 2, the research for the afore-mentioned United Nations Public Administration Country Studies involved reviewing legal and administrative procedures of those Member States with FOI provisions for giving access to information to the public. FOI provisions constitute commitments to accountability and define the parameters of trans-parency. They also serve as a basis for informed stakeholder engagement in formulating public policy and monitoring and evaluating the performance of the public sector.

FOI institutional developments con-stitute commitments to accountability and can define the parameters of transparency and responsiveness.

As reported in Chapter 2, 118 United Nations Member States have con-stitutional provisions on the right to information, with some even extending to access to public information, and 92 of the 118 have enabling FOI acts. An

---

101 Committee of Experts on Public Administration, Report from the 8th Session (see E./C.16/2009/5). Available from http://unpan1.un.org/intradoc/groups/public/docu-ments/un/unpan035088.pdf.

analysis and comparison of the FOI provisions, processes and timeframes show that 78 of the 92 Member States, or 85 per cent, include appeals mechanisms (see annex for additional information).

However, there is a need to go beyond the high-level statements made within laws or codes of conduct to establishing robust management and accountability systems. They should be based on an analysis of the results of good practices, including who is responsible for each positive contribution towards the desired outcome and who was driving the action-producing positive changes. These should be enhanced and good performance rewarded. Conversely, actions that are counterproductive should be scaled back, and those responsible for delivering them should be held accountable.

Organizational cultures that encourage learning, share information, exchange ideas, compare different ways of doing things and promote an attitude of enquiry through discussion, debate and problem-solving can break down institutional vertical silos. Together with more transparent and accountable institutions, this mindset also helps administrations to coordinate policies required to implement the 2030 Agenda for Sustainable Development. It can also encourage both adaptability to continuously changing challenges and accountability for results within public institutions. ◆

4. Shared and social accountability

The traditional way of ensuring accountability assumed that the majority of initiatives and actions were controlled by a single public agency. Yet, an increasingly complex reality has changed this paradigm. Traditional forms of vertical accountability for delegated authority must now be reconciled "with the need to operate through vast networks of organizations to achieve shared and collective results".[102] Nowadays, public institutions are "hubs of vast networks" and require "co-ordinated efforts of multiple actors" [103] to produce effective results.

The concept of accountability must take into consideration the shared responsibility of multiple agencies for shared results and government-wide priorities.[104] This poses several questions. How can the traditional hierarchi-

---

102 Jocelyne Bourgon, "A new synthesis of public administration, serving in the 21st century", Volume 81 of Queen's Policy Studies, McGill-Queen's Press, 2011.

103 Ibid.

104 Ibid.

cal accountability model or framework be adapted to environments where boundaries between public and private sectors are blurring, and where many players are involved in delivering services to meet citizen needs? In partnership arrangements between "equals", how can accountability be shared? In other words, how can hierarchical bureaucracies cope with services increasingly delivered through many and often non-government partners? For instance, the practice of contracting out to non-government partners is often used. Can existing laws and conventions ensure this new type of accountability?

In such circumstances, a new definition of accountability is needed that retains the essential features of traditional or hierarchical accountability but responds to the pressures of today, including more parties being involved in financing and delivering services. The Canadian Office of the Auditor General proposed the following definition:

Accountability is a relationship based on obligations to demonstrate, review, and take responsibility for performance, both the results achieved in light of agreed expectations and the means used.

> "Accountability is a relationship based on obligations to demonstrate, review, and take responsibility for performance, both the results achieved in light of agreed expectations and the means used."[105]

This definition encompasses accountability relationships between ministers and agency heads, departments or agencies of government, public servants in a hierarchical relationship and the executive and legislative branches, and among partners in delivery. The definition portends to enhance the traditional concept of accountability because it "allows for a shared accountability relationship among partners; encompasses reciprocal accountability of all parties in a delivery relationship; includes both ends and means; and the need for review and adjustment".[106]

The types of accountability relationships in an arrangement of shared responsibility include accountability among the partners; accountability between each partner and its own governing body, as in the case of a government to its parliament; and accountability to joint co-coordinating body that manages the arrangement.[107] In a federal system, accountability to the public may involve the central and subnational governments jointly agreeing to report to the public. Shared accountability may be more demanding of the partners involved.

---

105 Canada, Office of the Auditor General of Canada, Modernizing Accountability in the Public Sector, Chapter 9, Exhibits: 9.1, The elements of accountability in Report of the Auditor General of Canada, December 2002. Available from www.oag-bvg.gc.ca/internet/English/att_20021209xe01_e_12282.html.

106 Ibid.

107 Canada, Office of the Auditor General of Canada, Modernizing Accountability in the Public Sector Chapter 9, Main Points: 9.9 in Report of the Auditor General of Canada, December 2002. Available from www.oag-bvg.gc.ca/internet/English/att_20021209xe01_e_12282.html.

This framework can also be extended to cater to citizen engagement beyond the formal accountability framework because there is an expectation that inclusiveness will be integrated into policy and programme analysis and approaches.

Shared accountability issues were recently addressed in the Australian government's legislation on a new financial accountability framework.[108] In a position paper leading to the legislation, the Australian Department of Finance and Deregulation argued:

> "Although traditional vertical and hierarchical accountability models can provide efficiency and clear lines of accountability, they have limitations when it comes to dealing with many contemporary public policy issues that require action across several portfolios and sectors. Joined-up systems, which recognize the concepts of dual and multiple accountabilities, are needed to effectively address these issues."[109]

Government policies need to explicitly recognize, encourage and facilitate the implementation of shared accountability.

It is important to find adequate mechanisms so that accountability operates without leaving an "accountability deficit". Government policies need to explicitly recognize, encourage and facilitate the implementation of shared accountability. For instance, common reporting mechanisms need to replace or augment those addressed to the individual partnering agency or entity governing body. Also, accountability arrangements need to minimize on any trade-offs of efficiency. This is to say that compliance should not be an excessive burden that undermines public service or performance.

In the context of third party providers who engage with citizens, to whom should the service provider be accountable and how—to the citizen or to the funding body, or to both? What if there is more than one funding body? Do external audit organizations have the power to follow government funds into the operations of other levels of government and nongovernment third party providers?

Moreover, where many players are involved in service delivery, one can wonder whether public servants compromise their accountability if they exercise flexibility and are innovative in attempting to see that citizen needs are met. These issues come into sharp focus when implementation chains between governments and citizens are long and perhaps tangled. The chain can be too

---

108 Australia, Parliament of Australia, "Public Governance and Accountability Bill 2013", see Bibliography for detailed reference.

109 Australia, Department of Finance and Deregulation, Sharpening the Focus: A Framework for Improving Commonwealth Performance, Australian Government, November 2012.

complex for governments to exercise overall control, which can cause confusion and lowering of accountability standards.[110]

In sum, it is essential for the state and citizens to reshape public governance to maximize coherence and minimize tensions between accountability and efficiency; accountability and flexibility; accountability to other players both upwards and outwards; contractual and partnering arrangements between governments and other providers; and formal and informal mechanisms. They must also hold partners to account and learn from mistakes, while differentiating between blaming and learning. In the context of engaging citizens to ensure governments are held to account in delivering services, there can also be the need to balance the lengthy time it might take to engage citizens and the demands to get action on the grounds as quickly as possible.[111]

Both the 2008 World Public Sector Report[112] and the 2014 Report of the United Nations Committee of Experts on Public Administration[113] refer to the role of Supreme Audit Institutions (SAIs) to enhance public accountability. The 2008 World Public Sector Report argues that the capacity and coverage of external audit need to be expanded to address "weaknesses in overall political and civic governance arrangements, such as lack of access to information, shackled media, weak rule of law, and the pre-eminence of the executive over the legislative branch". According to the 2011 Report of the Expert Group Meeting held in Vienna,[114] SAIs are also "natural partners of citizens because they are impartial, independent, and strive to provide consumer-oriented audit services." Box 3.2 (page 64) describes an example of citizen collaboration with the State Audit Institution of Oman to detect administrative irregularities.

Citizens, through various formal and informal mechanisms, can hold the government to account. This is bottom-up accountability, which relies on civic engagement. Sometimes this is referred to as social accountability.

Citizens can exercise accountability formally through ombudsmen, report cards, citizen charters, watchdog committees, right-to-information laws, e-governance, mobile phones, Internet, etc.

---

110 Paul Posner, "Accountability challenges of third party government" in Lester Salamon (ed.), The Tools of Government, Oxford University Press, New York, 2002.

111 Meredith Edwards, "Participatory governance", Issues Paper No. 6, Corporate Governance Australian Research Council Project, University of Canberra, March 2008.

112 United Nations World Public Sector Report 2008, "People matter: civic engagement in public governance".

113 United Nations, Report on the Thirteenth Session of the Committee of Experts on Public Administration, New York, 7-11 April, 2014 (see E/2014/44-E/C.16/2014/6). Available from http://workspace.unpan.org/sites/Internet/Documents/UNPAN92994.pdf.

114 United Nations Department of Economic and Social Affairs Report of the Expert Group Meeting, Engaging Citizens to Enhance Public Sector Accountability and Prevent Corruption in the Delivery of Public Services, New York, 7-8 July 2011, Available from http://unpan1.un.org/intradoc/groups/public/documents/un-dpadm/unpan046544.pdf.

It is also defined as diagonal accountability because it involves citizens who are actors in a vertical accountability arrangement as well as in some form of horizontal accountability arrangement.

Box 3.2: **Oman—Complaints Window**

1st Place Winner of 2013 UNPSA (Category: Preventing and Combating Corruption in the Public Service, Region: Western Asia)

Description: Improving accountability and transparency through strengthening auditing of public institutions. This Complaint Window contributed to detection of administrative and financial irregularities.

Problem: 220 government entities are auditable by the State Audit Institution (SAI) in Oman. In addition, SAI has the authority to audit private companies in which the government has a stake of more than 51 per cent. However, SAI was limited to conducting financial audits of organizations and companies and to issuing recommendations without a mandate to enforce and monitor. The responsibility to implement the recommendations made by SAI would be solely with the audited entities, limiting its overall effectiveness. There were also no effective channels for the public to submit their complaints. Citizens were required to report their complaints and feedback in person in Muscat.

Solution: SAI was reformed to strengthen its mandate to conduct financial and administration audits in all fields. It also received a mandate to audit all accounts of government entities and private companies. SAI was empowered to enforce recommendations and implement changes in the audited organizations and could also issue penalties. In addition, a Department of Social Community (DSC) was established to enhance the relationship between SAI and the community. DSC's key functions include collating, registering, tracking and monitoring of public feedback, concerns and complaints through various channels. Through the SAI portal, the public can submit their complaints, feedback or concerns as well as the necessary related documentation. SAI can also be contacted via a variety of channels.

Impact: The initiative has improved the public's trust in government to reduce corrupt actions or malpractices and to ensure transparency and accountability of government entities. 400 cases of feedback from the public were registered since the launch of the electronic feedback/compliance system in July 2011. SAI conducted a total of 350 audits as compared to 177 audits in 2009/10. From 2010 to 2011, approximately 1.3 billion OMR (3.38 billion USD) of public funds were recovered. Most importantly, SAI was able to strengthen the level of transparency and accountability in the government entities, thus boosting public confidence in public service. 644 complaints were received between July 2011 and July 2013.

Method Used: financial and administration audits; accountability and transparency actions; prevention and eradication of corrupt actions; properly recording, handling and monitoring public complaints and feedback.

For more information: www.unpan.org/United Nations Public Service Awards.

Through exercising their voice, in theory at least, citizens can put pressure on governments to improve the quality of services delivered and to be accountable for meeting the expected results. Some specific ways that citizens can exercise accountability formally include ombudsmen, report cards, citizen charters, watchdog committees, right-to-information laws, e-governance, mobile phones and the Internet. Efforts to increase voice may not work, however, "without a parallel effort to build the effectiveness and capacity of state institutions to address growing demands and expectations". Cognizant that accountability is crucial for government performance, the Economic and Social Council of the United Nations recommended that Member States should "strengthen the cognitive and participatory capacities of their citizens; the professional and advisory capacities of intermediary organizations; and the learning and analytical capacities of governments and public managers".[115]

Access to information, particularly transparency in appraisal of expenditure in terms of allocation to priorities, assessment of value for money achieved and efficiencies in procurement, will demonstrate probity to the citizen. Perceptions of misuse of scarce resources in one area, e.g., large expensive cars belonging to government officials, will not build confidence in the financial management of other areas of public policy. Arguably, citizen engagement is meaningless if people do not have access to information and feel able to question, challenge and demand accountability without fear of reprisal.

A key precondition for effective citizen voice and accountability is that citizens be empowered by the State through the provision of information and that the significance of that information is understood. As noted in Chapter 2, 62 per cent of the United Nations Member States safeguard access to information through the inclusion of specific provisions in their constitutions. Not only is this considered essential for enabling citizen engagement, but also it is an indication of governments' disposition towards transparency.

A key precondition for effective citizen voice and demand for accountability is that citizens are empowered by the state through the provision of information and that the significance of that information is understood.

In 2013, the United Nations Committee of Experts on Public Administration underscored the need for governments not only to recognize the right to access but "engage in the proactive disclosure" of information. Recognizing this, more countries are recently moving from closed to more opened government and governance. An analysis of Data Protection Acts, currently in place, shows that in 78 countries (out of 82 countries with Data Protection Acts), provisions are made for information categories to which open data applies (See annex for additional information). The Committee further recommended that "no institutions supported by public funds should, a priori, be excluded from obligations to provide information. The judiciary must be capable of enforcing these rights and/or responsible institutions could be charged with guaranteeing implementation".[116]

Nevertheless, as discussed above, relationships and responsibilities regarding processes of accountability usually cannot be understood just by looking at the formal rules. The behaviour, abilities and expectations of both public service recipients and organizations that provide services matter greatly in understanding the implementation of a formal rule. The same formal rules

Relationships and responsibilities regarding processes of accountability usually cannot be understood just by looking at the formal rules.

---

115 Report of the Eighth Session of the Committee of Experts on Public Administration, New York 30 March–3 April 2009 (see E/2009/44–E./C.16/2009/5).

116 Report on the 12th Session of the Committee of Experts on Public Administration, New York, 15-19 April 2013 (see E/2013/44-E/C.16/2013/6). Available from www.unpan.org/DPADM/CEPA/12thSession/tabid/1544/language/en-US/Default.aspx.

can be interpreted very differently in varying contexts, influencing their implementation and, therefore, understandably, differences in the outcomes. Frameworks that include step-by-step guidelines on implementation procedures and administrative processes contribute to controlling such divergences.

The World Bank has developed an accountability framework, a "triangle of accountability", which includes three key service delivery relationships that can be strengthened in the interest of more effective accountability: citizens (and clients) influencing policy makers; policy makers influencing providers; and providers delivering services to citizens/clients. Core elements underpinning the World Bank's Citizen Voice and Accountability [117] approach include participation, inclusion, accountability and transparency.

Accountability can be exercised through the "short route", between citizens and government, or the "long route", through government to the service provider. Both routes will confront a lack of responsiveness or poor performance. How accountability operates will depend on how many providers are involved and whether citizens may find it difficult to work out who is responsible for what. The World Bank leans towards favouring the short route, although acknowledging that this may be at the cost of "supporting stronger and more accountable public institutions at all levels, especially in fragile states".[118]

Principles for effective social accountability include, among other factors, leadership's commitment, representation of broader segments of society, and interaction of formal and informal institutions.

Principles derived from relevant literature[119] for effective social accountability include many elements. Leadership's will to actively support open and free systems of accountability is required. Participatory processes open up accountability mechanisms to represent broader segments of society. Interaction of informal institutions with more recognized formal ones are needed, guided by factors such as flexibility of rules and existing cultural frameworks. Working as much as possible with existing institutions is more effective and efficient than creating new ones. Focusing capacity-building on political aspects as well as technical skills is necessary. It is important to take into account the time needed to get the desired results.

---

117 World Bank Group, Speech by President Jim Yong Kim, "Citizen voices: global conference on citizen engagement for enhanced development results", Washington, D.C., 13 March 2013. Available from www.worldbank.org/en/news/speech/2013/03/18/citizen-voices-global-conference-on-citizen-engagement-enhanced-development-results.

118 Stephen Commins, "Community participation in service delivery and accountability", Governance and Social Development Resource Centre, January 2007.

119 Wit de Joop and Akinyinka Akinyoade; Rocha Menocal, Alina and Sharma Bhavna, Joint Evaluation of Citizens' Voice and Accountability: Synthesis Report, GSDRC, November 2008; Ann Marie Goetz, and Rob Jenkins, "Hybrid forms of accountability: citizen engagement in institutions of public sector oversight in India", 2001.

In addition to legislation promoting transparency and accountability, key institutional characteristics or conditions for "effective state-citizen co-operation for improved accountability which have relevance for audit and other oversight institutions include: legal standing for non-governmental observers within institutions of public-sector oversight; a continuous presence for these observers throughout the process of the agency's work; well-defined procedures for the conduct of encounters between citizens and public-sector actors in meetings; structured access to the flow of official documentary information; and the right of observers to issue dissenting reports directly to legislative bodies".[120] ◆

5. E-government and open government data

It is increasingly recognized that e-tools enhance governments' information-sharing and interaction with citizens.[121] While providing enormous opportunities for transparency, accountability and anticorruption, e-government also represents many challenges (see also Chapter 2). E-government development is multidimensional and complex, requiring broad definition and understanding in order to design and implement successful vision and strategies. The challenges of e-government go far beyond technology. They call for organizational structures that respond to a whole-of-government approach along with new forms of leadership, transformative public and private partnerships, participatory processes and increased accountability. Nonetheless, these challenges need to be overcome by both developed and developing countries. Doing so will assist them to provide better and more accountable public services to their citizens and increase the chances of a more sustainable future by leveraging ICT.

E-tools enhance governments' interaction with citizens while strengthening information-sharing, transparency and accountability

The application of ICT to government service delivery and sharing of information helps to supplant hierarchical and bureaucratic structures with horizontal one-stop government network structures that facilitate customer orientation and increase transparency and accountability. Real-time tracking of service requests using ICT tools also enhances transparency and account-

---

120 Meredith Edwards, Accountable governance: modern accountability concepts, issues and principles, Draft Chapter 3, Contribution to World Public Sector Brief 2013 quoting Goetz and Jenkins (2001).

121 Report of the 8th Session of the Committee of Experts on Public Administration, New York 30 March–3 April 2009 (see E/2009/44–E./C.16/2009/5).

ability of public service delivery.[122] However, the use of ICT may come with some risks when governments use it to infringe peoples' right to privacy by engaging in unlawful surveillance over the Internet.

Box 3.3 (below) shows an example of enhanced transparency through a one-stop registration service for contractors tendering for public sector construction projects in Singapore. Given the important role of leaders in e-government —Chief Information Officers (CIOs) or "eLeaders"—and the institutional framework, DESA's research for UNPACS sought information on the level of CIOs and institutional settings of the highest decision-making office for e-government at the national level. The establishment of the CIO at different levels: ministerial, regulatory, advisory or technical, in sum, reflects the extent to which e-government is being prioritized nationally. The CIO at the highest political and executive level of a minister has a stronger influence and authority over e-government development. In comparison, the CIO as a technocrat heading a department or unit within a government ministry may lack both budgetary and human resources to successfully implement full-scale national e-government development strategies.

Box 3.3: Singapore—Contract Registry System (CRS), Building and Construction Authority

2nd Place Winner of 2012 UNPSA (Category: Preventing and Combating Corruption in the Public Service, Region: Asia and the Pacific)

Description: Improving registration service through a one-stop system for all contractors who wish to tender for public sector construction projects

Problem: With each agency having its own registration body and requirements, it was a costly exercise for the contractors who wanted to provide construction services for different government agencies.

Solution: CRS ensures that the registered companies have achieved a good track record, possess sufficient financial resources and employ a minimum pool of technical experts before they can tender for public sector projects.

Impact: The implementation of CRS has helped to promote transparency and an open and fair competitive business environment. This includes a very transparent and incorruptible way of measuring a contractor's capability and monitoring performance through feedback from the agencies that use the e-C41 Report and its online depository.

Method used: Registration to pre-qualify contractors to provide construction services to the public sector, saving time, resources and money for both the government agencies and the contractors. Standardized criteria are used by CRS to register all contractors which is available online to the public.

For more information: www.unpan.org/United Nations Public Service Awards.

---

122 E-government survey: e-government for the people (United Nations publication, Sales No. E.12.II.H.2).

Figure 3.1 (below) shows the distribution of CIO functions and institutions within the Member States across the four levels of the executive branch of government: ministerial, regulatory, advisory and technical. While research has been conducted on 193 United Nations Member States, UNPACS findings as of 2012 indicate that approximately 175 (or 91 per cent) have an identifiable e-government development coordinating authority (or CIO function).[123]

Figure 3.1 United Nations Member States' level of the chief information officers function

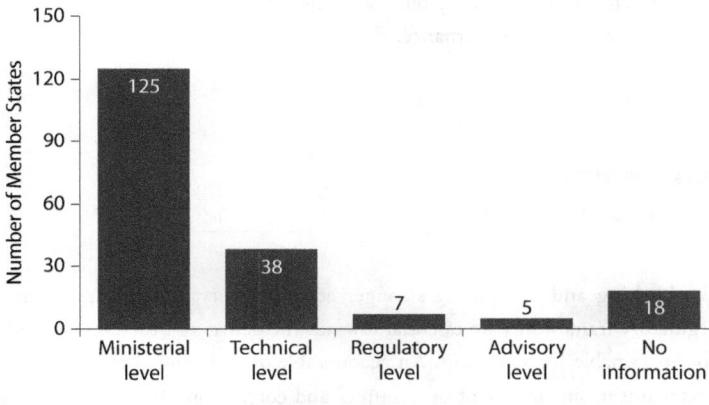

Source: United Nations Public Administration Country Studies.

The use of ICT also allows sharing government data with the wider public in open format. The concept is often referred to as "open government data", which has the three core elements of transparency, participation and collaboration with businesses and citizens. Opening up government data is fundamentally about more transparent and efficient use of resources and improving service delivery for citizens. By making much of its data available, while protecting the privacy of citizens and safeguarding national security, the government seeks to become more transparent and accountable. The effects of open data utilization are potentially far-reaching for sustainable development with positive impact on innovation, transparency, accountability, participatory governance and economic growth.

As part of their e-government strategies, over 60 governments around the world, which increasingly includes developing countries, have been open-

---

123 It must be noted that changes in CIOs as an institution are frequent. This may be attributable in part to the fact that the CIO as a government institutional structure is relatively new. The CIO function also changes to respond to contemporary overall institutional arrangements, such as the adoption of whole-of-government approaches.

ing previously "locked-up" government-held data sets, providing raw data to their citizens. Open government data is becoming an important government-provided raw information service that citizens can freely use, repurpose, create value out of and even co-produce. By fostering a culture of transparency, participation and collaboration, open data promotes the sharing of information and allows integration of economic, social and environmental data—often in an easily accessible, localized and visualized format.[124] The raw data can be turned into new informational products and services that not only stimulate private sector entrepreneurship but also monitor public sector performance and promotes accountable governance. ◆

6. Lessons learned

Establishing and integrating stronger accountability, anticorruption and regulatory frameworks are essential towards the delivery of the 2030 Agenda for Sustainable Development. An accountable organizational culture deters waste and mismanagement of resources and corruption. Accountability for performance serves to guide, monitor and evaluate public institutions and programmes, informing needed improvements. Building capacity for financial accountability is particularly important to building the trust for leveraging few resources and safeguarding new funds. However, this should go hand in hand with performance accountability.

Over the past two decades, reforms to increase accountability and to improve formal institutions and their enforcement often did not consider the political contexts in which reforms were being attempted. Certain types of informal institutions that are at odds with formal institutions cannot be immediately removed simply by attempting to enforce formal democratic accountability.[125] Some thought needs to be given to identifying and aligning formal institutions with informal ones to promote accountable governance.

---

124 E-government survey: e-government for the people (United Nations publication, Sales No E.12.II.H.2).

125 Mushtaq Husain Khan, Markets, States and Democracy: Patron-Client Networks and the Case for Democracy in Developing Countries, Democratization 12 (5) 2005, pp. 705-725; Douglass C. North., John J. Wallis, Steven B. Webb and Barry R. Weingast. "Limited access orders in the developing world: a new approach to the problem of development". World Bank Policy Research Paper No. 4359, World Bank: Washington, D.C., 2007.

Additional layers of complexity derive from the need to associate more than one agency and level of government in sharing the responsibility of service delivery. Yet, the old-fashioned way of ensuring accountability assumed that the majority of initiatives and actions were controlled by a single public agency. This clearly shows that traditional approaches of accountability are no longer sufficient because they need to be reconciled with shared responsibility of multiple agencies for shared results.

Against this backdrop, five principles for effective accountability that have been identified by the Office of the Auditor General of Canada as being a key to accountable governance:[126]

1. *Clear roles and responsibilities:* The decision-making roles and responsibilities of the parties in the accountability relationship should be well understood and agreed upon.

2. *Clear performance expectations:* The objectives pursued, the accomplishments expected and the operating constraints to action, which include means, operating principles and procedures, human resource management issues and adequate financial control should be explicit, understood and agreed upon.

3. *Balanced expectations and capacities:* Performance expectations should be clearly linked to and balanced with each party's capacities (authorities, skills and resources) to deliver.

4. *Credible reporting:* Credible and timely information should be reported to demonstrate what has been achieved, whether the means were appropriate and what has been learned (including reporting requirements, modalities, sufficient information for Parliament, etc.).

5. *Reasonable review and adjustment:* Fair and informed review and feedback on performance should be carried out by the parties, achievements and difficulties recognized, appropriate corrections made with appropriate consequences for the concerned individuals.

In addition, other actors (including the Australian National Audit Office) emphasize the importance of shared risk management, both in terms of delivery of services and the management of any contract.

Encouraging citizen-state relations is crucial for creating dialogue platforms that allow ordinary citizens or civil society organizations to hold government to account. A key precondition for effective citizen voice and accountability is that citizens be empowered by the state through the

---

126 Canada, Office of the Auditor General of Canada, "Principles of effective accountability". Available from www.oag-bvg.gc.ca/internet/English/att_20021209xe02_e_12283.html.

provision of information and that the significance of that information is understood. A key principle to assist social accountability to operate successfully is to have power relationships that permit an effective voice of citizens: linking Citizen Voice and Accountability[127] is meaningful only when citizens are powerful enough to make demands as well as those in positions of power being willing and having the capacity to respond.

SAIs and other independent oversight bodies, as part of the formal accountability structure, can provide valuable feedback and advice to assist public institutions to become more transparent and accountable. In addition, they are now developing the capacity to enhance social accountability mechanisms, taking into account specific country contexts.

Finally, it is important for governments to capitalize on the e-tools and open data potential to enhance their interaction with citizens in order to strengthen information sharing and participation, which contributes to more accountable governance.

Accountability denotes responsibility for results and outcomes, and not only processes. When operating effectively, it serves to ensure that public governance can flourish, related institutions perform well and services are delivered to citizens effectively and efficiently. These conditions will be essential to successfully implementing the new development agenda. ■

---

127 World Bank Group, speech by President Jim Yong Kim, "Citizen voices: global conference on citizen engagement for enhanced development results" Washington, D.C., 13 March 2013. Available from Citizen Voice and Accountability http://www. worldbank.org/en/news/speech/2013/03/18/citizen-voices-global-conference-on-citizen-engagement-enhanced-development-results.

Chapter 4

Transforming governance for the 2030 Agenda for Sustainable Development

1. The 2030 Agenda for Sustainable Development and governance

The preceding chapters addressed various aspects of the state and public administration capacity in public governance and development, stressing the value of responsiveness and accountability in both processes. While implementing policies and initiatives towards achieving the MDGs, the United Nations Member States have learned much about governance for development, particularly the importance of placing people at the centre. They have seen the importance of focusing on the needs of citizens and directly involving them in poverty eradication, as they look beyond 2015.

As stated by the United Nations Secretary-General Ban Ki-Moon, "By working together, we can reinvent government in ways that matter to ordinary people everywhere."[128] Indeed, since it has been adopted, the United Nations Millennium Declaration has been a source of inspiration and unity among world leaders and for public service professionals. They have been working in different regions to fulfil a set of catalytic objectives, agreed on as steps towards the eventual widespread achievement of the MDGs. Success in realizing the MDGs has not yet been even across and within countries. The world remained focused on the achievement of the MDGs until 2015, but it needs to ensure that progress is maintained beyond.

"By working together, we can reinvent government in ways that matter to ordinary people everywhere."

The MDGs have served as a global development framework since the turn of the millennium. As the target date for the goals approaches, preparations are under way to finalize the global development agenda beyond 2015 that embraces a sustainable development framework. The preparation includes discussions on how to enhance public governance in order to achieve the sustainable development goals.

Sustainable development is the subject of intense current interest in the United Nations. According to Our Common Future of the World Commission on Environment and Development[129] (or the 1987 Brundtland Report), sustainable development must meet the needs of the present generation without compromising the ability of future generations to meet their needs. Sustainable development emerged in response to concerns over existing unsustainable

---

128 United Nations Seventh Global Forum on Reinventing Government, Welcome Address by United Nations Secretary-General Ban Ki-Moon, Vienna, 26-27 June 2007. Available from www.unpan.org/DPADM/GlobalForum/7thGlobalForum/tabid/601/Default.aspx.

129 United Nations World Commission on Environment and Development (WCED), Our Common Future (also called Brundtland Report). Oxford, U.K.: Oxford University Press, 1987.

paths to development. It advocates a diversion from development trajectories that deplete and degrade natural resources and ecosystems that are bases for economic development. Sustainable development, in the context of the new development agenda, is also about behavioural change within societies, since de-emphasizing certain practices and motivating the use of alternative ones involve the introduction of new mindsets and behaviours at the societal level.

In some cases, such changes may impact production and consumption in key areas such as agriculture, transportation, construction and energy. The International Union for Conservation of Nature's (IUCN) Commission on Environmental Law noted that changes on such a scale will require goal-directed intervention by governments and other social actors, with the overall objective of reducing unsustainable activities and shifting the overall development trajectory onto more environmentally benign paths.

In June 2012 in Rio de Janeiro, the United Nations Member States renewed their commitment to an economically, socially and environmentally sustainable future for our planet and for present and future generations. They provided the basis for a single United Nations development agenda beyond 2015 with sustainable development at its core, supported by a set of internationally agreed SDGs.[130]

A little over two years after the Rio+20 conference, in August 2014, an Open Working Group on Sustainable Development Goals, composed of representatives of Member States, prepared a proposal for SDGs. Member States agreed that this proposal should be the main component of the new development agenda to be launched in September 2015. The Intergovernmental Committee of Experts on Sustainable Development Financing proposed options for a strategy to mobilize significant resources and the institutional governance mechanisms for their effective use, among other dimensions. The United Nations Secretary-General's Independent Expert Advisory Group on a Data Revolution for Sustainable Development (IEAG) highlighted the global challenges of dealing with gaps in what is known from data and gaps between those who have access to critical information and those who do not and proposals for dealing with those groups. These proposals served as critical inputs to the new development agenda to be adopted in a summit at the level of Heads of state and government in September 2015.

This is a time of uncommon opportunity for the international community to consider the question: how can government leaders and ordinary citi-

---

130 United Nations, Welcome address of Mr. Wu Hongbo, Under-Secretary-General for Economic and Social Affairs (DESA) and Secretary-General for the International Conference on Small Island Developing States at the 13th Session of the Committee of Experts on Public Administration (CEPA—http://workspace.unpan.org/sites/Internet/Documents/StatementUSG13thCEPA2014.docx.pdf.

zens transform governance and public administration for the new development agenda? There are no ready answers, but there are promising opportunities.

Government leaders have affirmed the importance of development framework, peace and security, good governance, the rule of law and the respect for human rights for a transformative sustainable development agenda. In particular, they point out that institutions at all levels that are effective, accountable and inclusive are needed.[131] But what does this mean in practice? How can policy-makers, tasked with transforming public institutions along these lines, be better equipped to address the complex challenges of the new framework for sustainable development?

The Rio+20 outcome document, agreed by all Member States, contains some crucial signposts. Public governance needs to assure the following:

1. Broad, active and meaningful participation in processes that contribute to decision-making, planning and implementation of policies and programmes for sustainable development at all levels. This implies the need for a strengthened civil society and enabling environment for participation of all stakeholders.[132]

2. Access to information. Improved access to ICT, especially broadband networks, is necessary, as are access to government proceedings, regulations, data and easy-to-understand procedures for accessing public services.[133]

3. National regulatory and policy frameworks that enable business and industry to advance sustainable development initiatives. Governments have a leading role to play in promoting partnerships in the public interest, responsible business practices and corporate social responsibility.[134]

4. Well-functioning institutions at all levels with a leading role for governments. Transparency and accountability mechanisms should be built into the fabric of public institutions—including in judiciaries and legislatures—as well as the capacity to achieve and demonstrate results.[135]

---

131 Outcome Document, Open Working Group for Sustainable Development, Goal 16, Sustainable Development Knowledge Platform: http://sustainabledevelopment.un.org/focussdgs.html.

132 United Nations, The Future We Want (A/CONF.216/1.1), 2012, paras. 13, 43 and 44.

133 Ibid., paras. 43 and 44.

134 Ibid., para. 46.

135 Ibid., paras. 10, 19 and 58c.

5. An integrated approach to planning and building sustainable cities and urban settlements. Support of local authorities and participation of urban residents in decision-making should be strengthened.[136]

6. Combatting corruption in all of its manifestations. All states should ratify or accede to the United Nations Convention against Corruption and proceed with its implementation.[137]

It is important to retain lessons learned in governance for what works and what does not in getting development results.

In transitioning from MDG endeavours to the new agenda, which embraces a sustainable development framework while retaining poverty eradication as an overriding objective, it is important to recall six dimensions of governance for getting development results. These six dimensions have already been discussed in various ways in chapters 2 and 3 but are also summarized in the next section. In addition, responsiveness and accountability are two key traits of governance that apply at all levels—including local, national or regional—and across the three dimensions of sustainable development—including economic, social or environmental. A successful transition from the MDGs to the new development agenda requires building political and social consensus through multi-sectoral integration and multi-stakeholder cooperation. ◆

2. Responsive and accountable governance for inclusive economic growth, social justice and environmental sustainability

Responsive and accountable governance are enabling conditions for economic growth, social inclusion and environmental sustainability.

Responsive and accountable governance for dealing with challenges of unsustainable debt burden and unequal economic growth, social inequalities and extreme poverty, and environmental degradation and climate change, to name a few, requires coherent public policies and new public sector capacities within efficient institutional and administrative frameworks. During the past decade, much progress towards achieving development goals is attributable to public sector reform.[138]

---

136 Ibid., paras. 134-136.

137 Ibid., para. 266.

138 See, for instance, United Nations Development Programme, Public Administration Reform, Practice Note, 2004 available at www.undp.org/content/dam/aplaws/publication/en/publications/democratic-governance/dg-publications-for-website/public-administration-reform-practice-note-/PARPN_English.pdf.

As identified in the Rio+20 conference, first, sustainability introduces a number of additional requirements to meaningful participation and active citizenship. An enabling environment for public participation emphasizes respect for human rights treaties, eradication of inequality and social exclusion, access and opportunities for all—both men and women. Active citizenship and democracy are interdependent, and what is needed is a sense of citizenship that incorporates duties with rights.

Second, these processes enabling participation can be strengthened when citizens, with no impediment, gain better access to public information, services and decision-making in development choices. They can be empowered through the civic right to information, which is enshrined in the constitution and legislation and enforced by information commissioners or similar offices. They can gain access to information through the application of ICT and simplified language. Citizens can have a stronger voice in economic and social councils that advise on allocating resources and identify development plans or in commissions that hear complaints.

Third, the leaders at Rio+20 emphasized that public-private partnerships and encouraged industry, interested governments and relevant stakeholders to develop models of best practice and facilitated action for the integration of sustainability reporting. This endeavour should take into account the experiences of already existing frameworks and pay attention to the needs of developing countries, including capacity-building. Overall, there was a recognition among the leaders that without the active involvement of private businesses and civil society in policy development and implementation, the pace of political action in furthering sustainable development could move neither as quickly nor as efficiently as the challenges warrant.

The active involvement of private businesses and civil society in policy development and implementation is needed to further sustainable development.

Fourth, governments need to strengthen institutional frameworks and capacities.[139] The redesign of related institutions for the 2030 Agenda for Sustainable Development, to accommodate desired cross-sector collaboration, can benefit from the application of ICT and experience gained through e-government reform. Public institutions can operate more transparently and with greater accountability by sharing information and encouraging public participation and oversight.

Fifth, governance in the new development framework has practical implications for influencing the future course of societal advancement by avoiding undesirable conditions and realizing specific goals.[140] This requires a measure of "societal self-steering", in which society collectively considers types

---

139 United Nations, A/67/769.

140 J. Meadowcroft, "Planning for sustainable development: what can be learned from the critics?" in M. Kenny and J. Meadowcroft (eds.), Planning for Sustainability. London, U.K.: Routledge, 1999, pp. 12-38.

*Innovative commu-
nication chan-
nels that connect
decision-makers and
their stakeholders
contribute to rais-
ing public demand
and expectations of
accountability.*

of futures that are most desirable and the route that should be avoided along the way. As earlier mentioned in this report, citizens—including men, women and members of all social groups—should be involved in decision-making to enhance governance responsiveness and accountability.

Finally, innovative communication channels that connect decision-makers and their stakeholders contribute to raising public demand and expectations of accountability. Combatting corruption in all of its forms is also important for safeguarding precious public resources and building public trust.

There is no universal formula to increase responsiveness and accountability across all sustainable development institutions. Appropriate policy development and implementation, responding to the needs of each specific context, can pave the way for integrating the three dimensions of sustainable development as well as key sectors. The Open Working Group on SDGs emphasized the need for promoting peaceful and inclusive societies for sustainable development, providing access to justice for all and building effective, accountable and inclusive institutions at all levels.[141] A more responsive and accountable governance is instrumental for ensuring inclusive economic growth, social justice and environmental sustainability. ◆

3. Development opportunities

As mentioned in Chapter 1, attaining SDGs requires addressing numerous challenges, first and foremost, eradicating extreme poverty. Other challenges include socioeconomic inequality; environmental degradation; unsustainable consumption and production patterns; lack of inclusive growth, decent employment and social protection; the need for increasing well-being beyond gross domestic product considerations; and inequitable power relations that limit social engagement.

Against these challenges, the Member States have agreed on 17 SDGs and 169 targets to be formally adopted in September 2015:

1. End poverty in all its forms everywhere
2. End hunger, achieve food security and improved nutrition, and promote sustainable agriculture

---

141 United Nations, Outcome Document, Open Working Group for Sustainable Development, Goal 16, Sustainable Development Knowledge Platform: http://sustainabledevelopment.un.org/focussdgs.html.

3. Ensure healthy lives and promote well-being for all at all ages

4. Ensure inclusive and equitable quality education and promote life-long learning opportunities for all

5. Achieve gender equality and empower all women and girls

6. Ensure availability and sustainable management of water and sanitation for all

7. Ensure access to affordable, reliable, sustainable and modern energy for all

8. Promote sustained, inclusive and sustainable economic growth, full and productive employment and decent work for all

9. Build resilient infrastructure, promote inclusive and sustainable industrialization and foster innovation

10. Reduce inequality within and among countries

11. Make cities and human settlements inclusive, safe, resilient and sustainable

12. Ensure sustainable consumption and production patterns

13. Tackle urgent action to combat climate change and its impacts

14. Conserve and sustainably use the oceans, seas and marine resources for sustainable development

15. Protect, restore and promote sustainable use of terrestrial ecosystems, sustainably manage forests, combat desertification, and halt and reverse land degradation and halt biodiversity loss

16. Promote peaceful and inclusive societies for sustainable development, provide access to justice for all and build effective, accountable and inclusive institutions at all levels

17. Strengthen the means of implementation and revitalize the global partnership for sustainable development

A shift towards a development that is people-centred, rights-based and towards greater inclusiveness and participatory decision-making is evidenced by the 17 proposals for SDGs.

These goals present opportunities for attaining sustainable development by also realizing the unfinished business of MDGs. The overriding priority is the eradication of poverty in all its forms everywhere. This remains as an "indispensable requirement for sustainable development".[142]

The increased attention to the above referenced 17 goals as development opportunities shows, as noted in Chapter 1, that there has been a shift towards development that is people-centred, rights-based and towards greater inclusiveness and participatory decision-making processes. The next section examines how governance responsiveness and accountability offer important opportunities in reaching long-lasting sustainable development outcomes. ◆

---

142 Ibid.

4. Governance opportunities

Previous WPSRs addressed challenges for designing governance reforms, particularly for achieving the MDGs, including globalization, e-government, human potential for better public sector performance and civic engagement. The 2015 WPSR addresses challenges for a more responsive and accountable governance for attaining the SDGs.

These challenges include ensuring institutional coherence and adapting institutions to the necessities of integrating economic, social and environmental pillars. They include harmonizing actions among different levels of government for enhanced responsiveness to peoples' needs and to foster public participation, transparency and accountability. Sustaining the appropriate use of technology also requires enabling regulatory frameworks and environments.

Governance opportunities exist for tackling sustainable development challenges.

In tackling these multiple challenges, it is important to recall the governance opportunities considered in previous chapters:

1. Well-functioning, effective and coherent public institutions at both central and subnational levels. This is ensured by robust transparency, performance management and accountability mechanisms, built into their fabric as well as the capacity to achieve and demonstrate effective results that respond to public needs. Public administration, serving as the bedrock of the rule of law and effective delivery of essential public services, is critical to development.

2. Public servants, starting from the leadership level, who display technical and professional capacities, professionalism, integrity, transparency, accountability, effectiveness and responsiveness in conducting public affairs and delivering public goods and services to all people. Their ability to achieve a deeper understanding of the diversity of people's needs, desires and aspirations and to develop effective relationships across public institutions and with non-state actors is essential for responsive and accountable action.

3. Appropriate regulatory frameworks that guide elected officials and public servants to behave in ways that meet public expectations and allow access to independent, responsive and innovative service delivery. They need to be accompanied by performance assessment mechanisms that focus on the quality, quantity, equity and promptness of services.

4. Broad, active and meaningful public participation in processes that contribute to decision-making, planning, implementation, monitoring and evaluation of policies and programmes at all levels. This requires a strengthened civil society and an enabling environment for participation of all stakeholders—including men, women and

members of all social groups. Public engagement is more likely to lead to policies that have greater impact, not only sectorally but also at an integrated level. It also is more likely to attain desired results by tapping into the knowledge and experience of local communities. It can also create dialogue platforms that allow ordinary citizens and civil society organizations to hold government to account.

5. The application of ICT and experience gained through e-government reform for greater efficiency, cost effectiveness, quality, responsiveness, expanded reach, speed and accessibility of public services. These opportunities go beyond technology, encompassing organizational structures and skills, new forms of leadership, transformative public and private partnerships, and innovative communication channels. They connect decision-makers and their stakeholders, fostering stronger civic engagement through e-participation. It is important for governments to capitalize on e-tools and open data potential to strengthen dialogue, information-sharing, transparency and accountability.

6. Free and timely public access to reliable information. Access to government proceedings, regulations and data of public interest, an enabling environment in terms of comprehensive legal and institutional frameworks, structures and processes, complemented by capacity building also contribute to combatting corruption in all of its forms. This has positive effects on safeguarding public resources and building public trust.

7. New accountability frameworks that reconcile traditional approaches with increasingly shared responsibility of multiple agencies for shared results. Measures to increase transparency and accountability ensure that public resources are deployed for their intended purposes and decisions are made in the best public interest. SAIs and other independent oversight bodies, also in partnership with citizens, can provide valuable feedback and advice towards greater transparency and accountability. Effective new frameworks require maximizing coherence between accountability and efficiency; accountability and flexibility; and accountability with non-state actors.

These opportunities are closely associated with the way the state plays a role in the socio-politico-economic development of the people. Seizing these opportunities is critical for the state to be an effective enabler for the implementation of the new development priorities. This is also reaffirmed by the fact that the Member States consider "good governance, the rule of law and human rights" as "essential for sustained, inclusive and equitable economic growth, sustainable development and the eradication of poverty and hunger".[143] ◆

5. Lessons for transformative actions

Public administration needs to be effective, efficient, economic, transparent, accountable, equitable and responsive to the needs of the public. It also needs to embrace participation.

Governance is transformative only when it is more responsive to overcome the daunting, interconnected and increasingly complex challenges necessary to attain sustainable development for all. Policies, strategies, programmes, activities and resources need to be coherent. They also need to revolve around people's real needs with a firm commitment to "leave no one behind". What is the full range of transformative action required for responding to emerging development priorities? No single answer applies to the gamut of development contexts which present a varying mix of development and governance opportunities and related challenges.

One element is already clear. Although private businesses, civil society organizations and individuals (in their capacity as consumers and as citizens) all have important roles to play in orienting societal transformation, the contribution of governments is central. As the United Nations Secretary-General stated in 2014, "Effective governance for sustainable development demands that public institutions in all countries and at all levels be inclusive, participatory and accountable to the people".[144] Governments need to focus on satisfying people's expectations in terms of quality, quantity and promptness of the public services. They should also ensure access to them based on principles of equality and equity.

As noted earlier, public administration has a central position in the practice of public management and good governance. Public administration also needs to be in its institutions, structures, systems, procedures, processes, networks, relationships, practices, approaches and methods of work, as well as leadership behaviour effective, efficient, economic, transparent, accountable, equitable and responsive to the needs of the public. However, its core functions need to be redefined with a focus on justice and security, regulatory control and the delivery of services which are critical to the process of sustainable development including education, health and environmental protection.

---

143 Ibid, para. 12.

144 United Nations General Assembly, "The road to dignity by 2030: ending poverty, transforming all lives and protecting the planet", synthesis report of the Secretary-General on the post-2015 sustainable development agenda, A/69/700, 2014, para. 77, p. 19.

Past experience has shown that transformative governance will entail bringing together the best attributes of public administration, public management and governance to construct a sharp instrument for effective, efficient, responsive, transparent, and accountable functioning of the state. Each country needs to search for a response vis-à-vis the breadth of transformative action to be undertaken.

Responsive public policies and programmes are likely to be adopted by Member States that successfully engage and consistently take into account needs expressed by various social groups. This Report argues that trust, cooperation and increased public participation in decision-making are critical components of transformative capacities needed to achieve development priorities.

Multi-stakeholder processes offer opportunities to gather information and understanding from many actors to set appropriate reform trajectories and implement solutions. They enable greater mobilization of knowledge and resources and allow for a higher level of public participation in various developmental initiatives. This requires active engagement by both civil society and the private sector.

Engagement of all stakeholders at various administrative levels, including local authorities and communities, is critical. This allows for consensus-building in development planning and management as well as reducing competition and conflict among different levels of government. However, multi-stakeholder partnerships require mutual accountability to be reconciled with shared responsibility of multiple actors and agencies for shared results and shared risk management.

Greater accountability requires the engagement of independent oversight institutions such as supreme audit institutions and external actors including civil society organizations and ordinary citizens. Encouraging citizen-state relations is crucial for creating dialogue platforms that allow the public to hold government to account. Nevertheless, linking Citizen Voice and Accountability[145] is meaningful only when citizens are powerful enough to make demands and when those in positions of power are willing and have the capacity to respond.

Having better access to information is another crucial element. On the one hand, better information allows for evidence-based decision-making through analysis of relevant data. On the other, public agencies will be subject to much more intensive oversight and second-guessing by legislators and

---

145 World Bank Group, Speech by President Jim Yong Kim, "Citizen voices: global conference on citizen engagement for enhanced development results", Washington, D.C., 13 March 2013. Available from 's Citizen Voice and Accountability http://www.worldbank.org/en/news/speech/2013/03/18/citizen-voices-global-conference-on-citizen-engagement-enhanced-development-results.

stakeholders.[146] This requires changing the way they gather and disseminate information for better knowledge management and more collective decision-making, particularly at the local level.

It is important for governments to capitalize on the e-tools and open data potential to enhance their interaction with citizens in order to strengthen information sharing and participation, which contributes to more accountable governance. ICT provides a platform to better integrate and accelerate economic, social and environmental dimensions of sustainable development. The transformative potential of using technology in government can reduce counterproductive tendencies towards "silos" that isolate public officials and their departments,[147] thereby stimulating integration and coordination within government.

ICT provides a platform to better integrate and accelerate delivery of all three pillars of sustainable development.

ICT utilization can also expand the reach and efficiency of public organizations and their connection with stakeholders;[148] it has the potential to enhance information exchange as well as transparency, responsiveness and accountability. Shared value frameworks among parties can influence the enrichment of these developments for the common good and to foster social innovation.[149]

Yet, it is important to recall that networks of organizations across sectors include those functioning under both formal and informal systems. Differences in organizational cultures in the public sector, the private sector and civil society may influence operational arrangements and behaviour patterns that inhibit cooperation and affect the legitimacy of public decision-making. Attaining coherence among formal and informal organizations within society is critical. Mapping informal systems and aligning them with formal systems would better foster collaboration processes and reduce the undermining of consensus-building. Shared accountability frameworks also need to incorporate carefully planned incentive systems.

In conclusion, working towards a vision of sustainable development within the context of the new development agenda can benefit from effectively addressing interrelationships, citizen engagement at national and sub-national

---

146 John O. McGinnis, Accelerating democracy: transforming governance through technology, Princeton University Press: Princeton, New Jersey, 2012.

147 A Dale, At the Edge. Vancouver: University of British Columbia Press 2001.

148 The Internet Governance Forum (IGF) is an example of social innovation. Through its secretariat, IGF provides policy dialogue space and promotes the exchange of knowledge and information. It also builds capacity of the stakeholders, especially from developing countries, to learn about the potential of the Internet. Further information available from www.intgovforum.org/cms/.

149 To this end, the digital divide, capacity deficits, Internet governance, cybersecurity and respect for privacy should be addressed.

levels, responsive and accountable governance institutions, technical innovation including knowledge-sharing and multi-stakeholder engagement to forge partnerships for sustainable development. Governance for sustainability must be innovative, proactive and inclusive rather than routine, theoretical, reactive and divisive. Governments should exercise leadership in more sustainable policy delivery and practices for more sustainable futures.[150] ■

---

150 The Centre for Sustainable Development, University of Westminster and the Law School, University of Strathclyde Sustainable Development: A Review of International Literature. Scottish Executive Social Research: Scotland, 2006, p. 126.

Annex—
Technical note

The United Nations Public Administration
Country Studies (*UNPACS*)

UNPACS is being created as a knowledge base to assist the 193 United Nations Member States[151] in enriching their capacities to deliver high-quality public services that are efficient, effective, transparent, accountable, resistant to corruption and citizen-centred. As a resource readily available online, it is intended to support governments and all other stakeholders in making evidence-based decisions for the implementation of internationally agreed development agendas.

With the aim of creating UNPACS, the Department of Economic and Social Affairs of the United Nations, through its Division for Public Administration and Development Management (DESA/DPADM), is collecting and analysing information on conventional and emerging topics related to public administration. A set of research questions has been developed specifically to target the research topics and guide individual research teams. Collection of information is done primarily through Internet research of the websites of national government agencies. Official publications are another source of information. The information collected for this research is categorized into four areas. The first, regulatory frameworks, include national constitutions, legislation and public policies and organizational administrative issuances such as codes of conduct. Second, the organizational framework focuses on Member States' public administrative bodies such as the institutions and leading governmental officials and their capacities to influence public administration. Third, channels and modalities are taken into consideration as they relate to service delivery and implementation. Fourth, case studies of good practices by the Member States—within their national and regional frameworks and according to the international agreements to which they are partied—are presented.

The following three specific themes have guided the research in 2012: 1) government institutions and human resources development; 2) electronic and mobile government; and 3) citizen engagement in managing development and public accountability. Comparative public administration country profiles for the 193 Member States are in the process of being assembled, in order to provide government policymakers and the public with access to comparative information on the policies, legal and institutional frameworks, and practices which governments around the world apply. Findings of DESA/DPADM research on each of the aforementioned topics have been aggregated and captured in charts presented in some chapters of the 2015 World Public Sector Report, to illustrate Member States' activities. For example, they are presented for freedom of access to information acts (FOIA), e-government development

---

151 List available at: www.un.org/en/members/.

policies and aspects of public sector reform such as public service codes of conduct that assist Member States in promoting professionalism, integrity and ethics in governance and public administration.

The UNPACS data source is the collection of documents, relating to each topic, that is available from 193 UN Member States. Primary sources of information are these documents from official government websites of the Member States, including of the sites of the national government, parliament, the president's office or other ministries as well as supreme courts or constitutional courts. If no official government site provides documentation in English or another United Nations official language, secondary sources by reputable institutions are consulted. In order to have sources as uniform as possible for the analysis and in order to prevent language and translation issues, English sources were given priority. In the event of doubts or discrepancies, and where possible, the original language documents were also analysed using translations from reputable sources on in-house translations.

Basic statistics are deduced primarily from analysing individual data sets on the Member States together and presented by region. As data on the areas of focus increases, more in depth analysis will be available. DESA/DPADM will also develop assessment toolkits and online training materials for the Member States, based on UNPACS research. In this technical note, an overview of preliminary research findings is shown for data up to 31 December 2012 for each of the thematic areas listed above. ◆

1. Government institutions and human resources development

To analyse the framework for managing conduct in the public service in the United Nations Member States, research was undertaken to explore the common values stated in various pieces of legislation and administrative issuances. They include codes of ethics, codes of conduct and civil service laws. The aim of the research was to analyse the basic common values and standards of conduct, which are considered important for the proper functioning of the public service. Research findings, shown in Figure 5.1, can be used as a checklist or a general guide in the development of new code(s) of conduct/ethics as well as regional or model codes of conduct/ethics.

Figure 5.1 United Nations Member States listing values/ principles for proper public service functioning (shown as a

percentage of 101 UN Member States in the region with codes or standards of conduct, ethics or equivalent)

101 Member States have codes or standards of conduct, ethics or equivalent. Content analysis shows that "professionalism" as a value is stated more

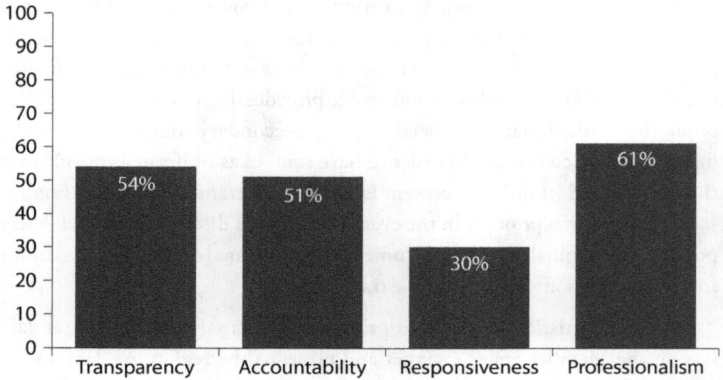

frequently than other values. ◆

2. Electronic and mobile government

National policies on e-government development were researched and e-government coordinating authorities, including their highest public officials, chief information officers (CIOs) or equivalent at the national level, were compiled. The availability of data about e-government coordinating authorities for 193 Member States, whether it is one particular ministry, more than one ministry, a coordinating body, or several entities, can provide a basis for analysing effective decision-making processes. Research on e-government development has continued over the past decade as part of the DESA/DPADM e-government development programme. It is published in the biennial United Nations E-Government Surveys,[152] a flagship publication of DESA/DPADM. Figure 5.2.1 (page 154) consists of six components to show how many Member States have national strategies and policies on e-government. This is displayed

152   See www.unpan.org/e-government.

in each of the five world regions. (YES indicates existing policy and NO indicates no policy.)

Figure 5.2.1i **United Nations Member States in Africa with and without national policies on e-government development (shown as a percentage of 54, i.e., the total number of UN Member States in the region)**

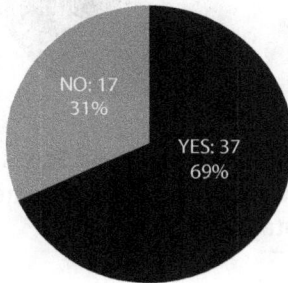

Figure 5.2.1ii **United Nations Member States in the Americas with and without national policies on e-government development (shown as a percentage of 35)**

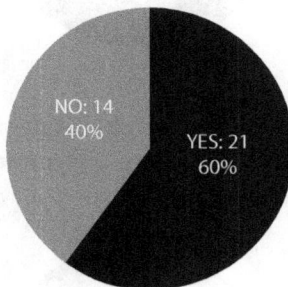

Figure 5.2.1iii **United Nations Member States in Asia with and without national policies on e-government development (shown as a percentage of 47)**

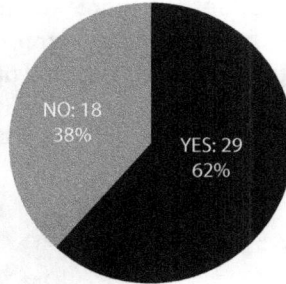

Figure 5.2.1iv **United Nations Member States in Europe with and without national policies on e-government development (shown as a percentage of 43)**

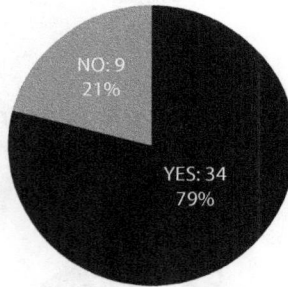

Figure 5.2.1v **United Nations Member States in Oceania with and without national policies on e-government development (shown as a percentage of14)**

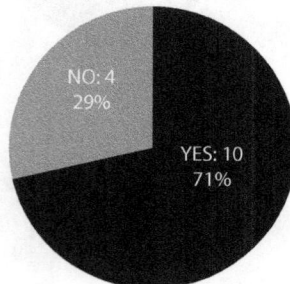

Figure 5.2.1vi **United Nations Member States with and without national policies on e-government development**

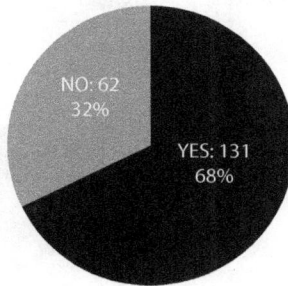

---

3. Citizen engagement in managing development

The overall purpose of this section is to provide government policymakers and citizens with easy access to comparative information on the policy, regulatory and organizational frameworks which governments around the world apply in engaging their citizens in managing development. The research aims at analysing three building blocks of citizen engagement that Member States can provide: 1) giving access to information to citizens, 2) initiating consultation with citizens to solicit feedback on issues that might concern them, and 3) engaging citizens in decision-making, more integrally, interactively and jointly with itself and other relevant actors. Findings as of 31 December 2012 on the first two building blocks are contained in the figures below.

Figure 5.3.1i **United Nations Member States with freedom of information acts (grouped by region)**

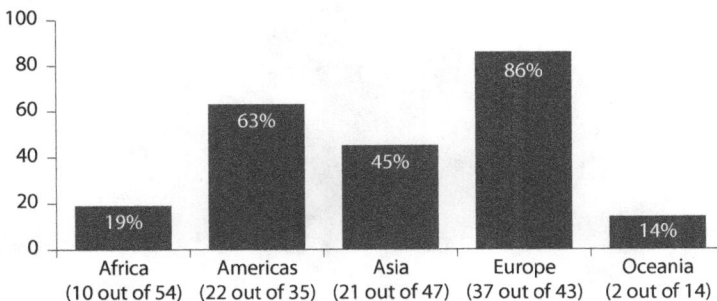

Figure 5.3.1ii **United Nations Member States which recognize citizens' rights to access information in national constitutions (total: 193 Member States)**

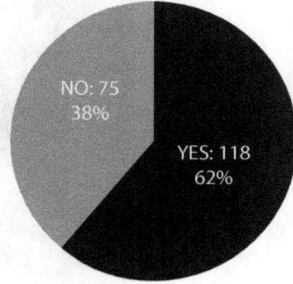

NO: 75
38%

YES: 118
62%

Figure 5.3.1iii **United Nations Member States which refer to citizen engagement in the freedom of information acts (total: 92 Member States with FOIA)**

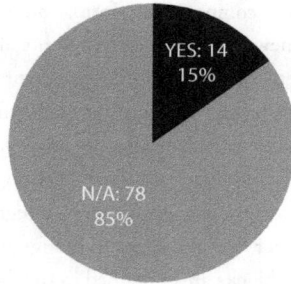

YES: 14
15%

N/A: 78
85%

Figure 5.3.1iv **United Nations Member States which provide information in multiple languages within freedom of information acts (total: 92 Member States with FOIA)**

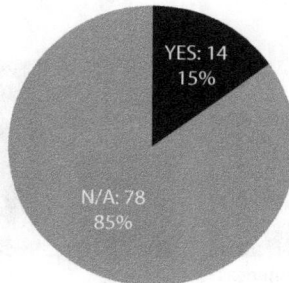

YES: 14
15%

N/A: 78
85%

Figure 5.3.1v **UN Member States which provide appeal mechanisms within freedom of information acts (by Member State; total: 92 Member States with FOIA)**

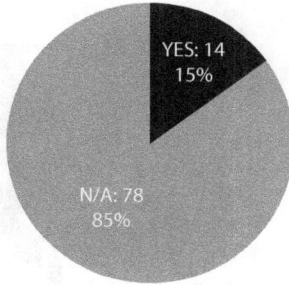

Figure 5.3.1vi **United Nations Member States where the freedom of information act contains a timeframe for providing access to public information (total: 92 Member States with FOIA)**

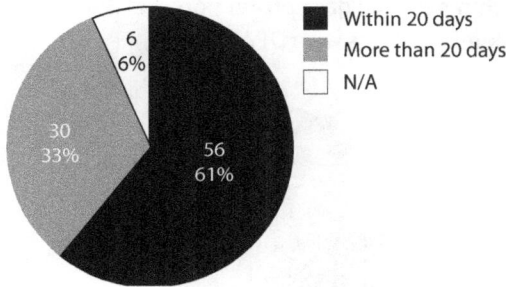

Figure 5.3.2 **United Nations Member States which have legislation concerning economic and social councils or similar institutions**

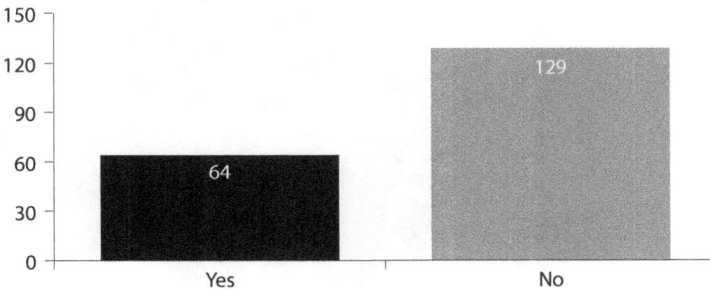

Figure 5.3.3i **United Nations Member States which have national data protection acts (grouped by world region; total: 193 Member Sates)**

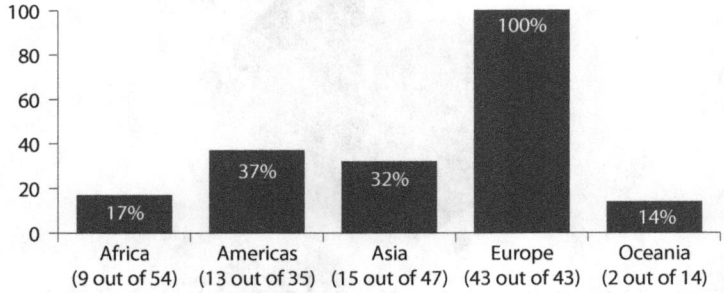

| | Africa
(9 out of 54) | Americas
(13 out of 35) | Asia
(15 out of 47) | Europe
(43 out of 43) | Oceania
(2 out of 14) |

Figure 5.3.3ii **United Nations Member States which include provisions for information categories to which open data applies within national data protection acts (by Member States; total: 82 Member States with DPA)**

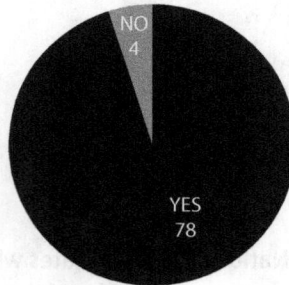

Bibliography

Alford, John, and Janine O'Flynn, *Rethinking Public Service Delivery*, Palgrave Macmillan (2012).

Australian Public Service Commission, *Delivering Performance and Accountability, Contemporary Government Challenges Series*, (Commonwealth of Australia, 2009).

Australian Public Service Commission, *Policy Implementation through Devolved Government, Contemporary Government Challenges Series*, (Commonwealth of Australia, 2009).

Ayres, I., and J. Braithwaite, *Responsive Regulation: Transcending the Deregulation Debate*, (Oxford University Press, 1992), New York.

Bourgon, Jocelyne, *A New Synthesis of Public Administration, Serving in the 21st Century*, volume 81 of Queen's Policy Studies, (McGill-Queen's Press, 2011).

Byström, Marie, "Formal and informal systems in support of farmer management of agrobiodiversity: some policy challenges to consolidate lessons learned", CAPRi *Working Paper No. 31*, (International Food Policy Research Institute, 2004), http://www.capri.cgiar.org/pdf/capriwp31.pdf.

Commins, Stephen, "Community participation in service delivery and accountability", Governance and Social Development Resource Centre, (January 2007).

Craig W. Thomas, "Maintaining and restoring public trust in government agencies and their employees", *Administration & Society*, No. 30, (1998), pp. 166-193.

Dale, A., *At the Edge*, (University of British Columbia Press, 2001), Vancouver.

Edwards, M., "Participatory governance", Issues Paper No. 6, Corporate Governance ARC Project, University of Canberra (March 2008).

Fukuyama, Francis, *The Origins of Political Order: From Prehuman Times to the French Revolution*, (Farrar, Straus and Giroux, 2011), New York.

Global Financial Integrity, *Global Financial Integrity Report*, (December 2012) http://iff.gfintegrity.org/iff2012/2012report.html.

Goetz, Ann Marie, and Rob Jenkins, "Hybrid forms of accountability: citizen engagement in institutions of public sector oversight in India", *Public Management Review*, volume 3, Issue 3, (2001).

Khan, Mushtaq Husain, "Markets, states and democracy: patron-client networks and the case for democracy in developing countries," *Democratization*, volume 12, Issue 5, (2005).

Khor, Martin, "Knowledge towards solutions", *Perspectives on Institutional Frameworks for Sustainable Development*, Speaking Notes at UNDESA/Indonesian Government high level dialogue on institutional framework for sustainable development, (2011), www.planetunderpressure2012.net.

Kikuchi, M., "Assessing government efforts to (re)build trust in government: challenges and lessons learned from Japanese experiences", *Research in Public Policy Analysis and Management*, (2008), volume 17.

Kim, S., "Public trust in government in Japan and South Korea: does the rise of critical citizens matter?" *Public Administration Review*, (2010), September-October.

Levi, M., and L. Stoker, "Political trust and trust worthiness", *Annual Review of Political Science*, No. 3, (2002).

McGinnis, John O., *Accelerating Democracy: Transforming Governance through Technology*, (Princeton University Press, 2012), New Jersey.

Mead, Walter Russell, "Accelerating democracy: transforming governance through technology", *Foreign Affairs*, volume 92, Issue 3, Council on Foreign Affairs, (Gale, Cengage Learning, 2013).

Meadowcroft, James, "Planning for sustainable development: what can be learned from the critics?" in M. Kenny and J. Meadowcroft, eds., *Planning for Sustainability*, (Routledge, 1999), London, U.K.

Mulgan, Richard, *Holding Power to Account: Accountability in Modern Democracies*, Palgrave Macmillan (2003).

North, Douglass C., John J. Wallis, Steven B. Webb and Barry R. Weingast, "Limited access orders in the developing world: a new approach to the problem of development", *World Bank Policy Research Paper No. 4359*, (World Bank, 2007), Washington, D.C.

North, Douglass C., John J. Wallis, Steven B. Webb and Barry R. Weingast, eds., *In the Shadow of Violence: Politics, Economics and the Problems of Development*, (Cambridge University Press, 2013), Cambridge.

Office of the Auditor General of Canada, December Report of the Auditor General of Canada, Chapter 9, "Modernizing accountability in the public sector", Exhibits: 9.1—The elements of accountability, (2002), http://www.oag-bvg.gc.ca/internet/English/att_20021209xe01_e_12282.html.

Office of the Auditor General of Canada, *December Report of the Auditor General of Canada*, Chapter 9, "Modernizing accountability in the public sector," Main Points — 9.9., (2002), http://www.oag-bvg.gc.ca/internet/English/att_20021209xe01_e_12282.html.

Parliament of Australia, "Public governance, performance and accountability bill 2013," Revised Explanatory Memorandum, Senate, (2013).

Posner, Paul L., "Accountability challenges of third party government", in Lester Salamon, ed., *The Tools of Government*, Oxford University Press (2002), New York.

Quermonne, Jean-Louis (1991), "L'appareil administratif de l'Etat", Editions du Seuil, Paris.

Rocha Menocal, Alina, and Sharma Bhavna, "Joint evaluation of citizens' voice and accountability: synthesis report", *Governance, Social Development, Humanitarian, Conflict*, (GSDRC, 2008) November.

Scholz, J. T., and M. Lubell, "Trust and taxpaying: testing the heuristic approach to collective action," *American Journal Of Political Science* (1998), volume 42.

Sabel. Charles F., and Jonathan Zeitlin, eds. (2011) *Experimentalist Governance in the European Union: Towards a New Architecture*, Blackwell Publishing Ltd. ISBN 978-0-19-957249-6.

Senge, Peter M., *The Fifth Discipline: The Art & Practice of The Learning Organization*, (Doubleday: revised and updated edition, 2006).

The Broadband Commission for Digital Development, *Transformative Solutions for 2015 and Beyond a Report of the Broadband Commission Task Force on Sustainable Development*, (2013), http://www.broadbandcommission.org/documents/working-groups/bb-wg-taskforce-report.pdf.

The Centre for Sustainable Development, University of Westminster and the Law School, University of Strathclyde, *Sustainable Development: A Review of International Literature*. Scottish Executive Social Research, (2006) Scotland.

Thomas, C., "Maintaining and restoring public trust in government agencies and their employees", *Administration & Society*, No. 30, (1998).

Tolbert, C., and K. Mossberger, "The effects of e-government on trust and confidence in Government," *Public Administration Review*, No. 66, (2006).

Tyler, Tom R., *Why People Obey the Law*, (Yale University Press, 1990) New Haven, CT.

United Nations, "A new global partnership: eradicate poverty and transform economies through sustainable development", *Report from the High-Level Panel of Eminent Persons on the Post-2015 Development Agenda*, (2013), http://www.post2015hlp.org/wp-content/uploads/2013/05/.

United Nations, *A 60-Year History: The Contribution of the United Nations to the Improvement of Public Administration*, (2008), http://www.unpan.org/DPADM/History/SectionIVTheevolutionoftheUnitedNations/tabid/125i2/language/en-US/Default.aspx.

United Nations, "A world that counts: mobilising the data revolution for sustainable development", *Report of the Secretary-General's Independent Expert Advisory Group on a Data Revolution for Sustainable Development (IEAG)*, (2014).

United Nations, Commission on Social Development, *Report on the Fifty-second Session*, E/2014/26-E/CN.5/2014/10 (2014).

United Nations, Committee of Experts on Public Administration, *Compendium of Basic Terminology in Governance and Public Administration* E/C.16/2006/4, (2016) http://unpan1.un.org/intradoc/groups/public/documents/un/unpan022332.pdf.

United Nations, Committee of Experts on Public Administration, *Report on the 12th Session* E/2013/44-E/C.16/2013/6, (2013), http://www.unpan.org/DPADM/CEPA/12thSession/tabid/1544/language/en-US/Default.aspx.

United Nations, Committee of Experts on Public Administration, *Report on the Thirteenth Session*, E/2014/44-E/C.16/2014/6), (2014), http://workspace.unpan.org/sites/Internet/Documents/UNPAN92994.pdf.

United Nations, Committee of Experts on Public Administration, *Report on the 8th Session* E./C.16/2009/5, (2009), http://www.unpan.org/8thSession/tabid/835/Default.aspx.

United Nations, Committee of Experts on Public Administration, Revitalizing Public Administration as a Strategic Action for Sustainable Human Development: an

Overview, E/C.16/2004/2, (2004), http://unpan1.un.org/intradoc/groups/public/documents/un/unpan015105.pdf.

United Nations Commission on Sustainable Development Secretariat, "Current ideas on sustainable development goals and indicators", *Rio 2012 Issue Briefs No. 6. Rio+20*, (United Nations Conferences on Sustainable Development, 2013), para. 2.

United Nations, 7th Global Forum on Reinventing Government, Building Trust in Government, *Welcome Address by United Nations Secretary General Ban Ki-Moon*, (Vienna, 2008), http://www.unpan.org/DPADM/GlobalForum/7thGlobalForum/tabid/601/Default.aspx.

United Nations, Qian, Haiyan, Video Message, Experts Group Meeting on Citizen Engagement in Post 2015 Development Agenda (3-4 December 2012), Beirut, Lebanon.

United Nations, Qian, Haiyan, Video Message from Ms. Haiyan Qian on the occasion of the Capacity Development Workshop on "*Citizen Engagement and the Post-2015 Development Agenda*" held in Beirut, Lebanon, (5-6 December 2012) http://www.youtube.com/watch?v=D1Pynb3cfDA.

United Nations Development Programme, and Office of the High Commissioner of Human rights, *Global Thematic Consultation, on Governance and the Post 2015 Development Framework: Consultation Report*, (2013) http://www.worldwewant2015.org/governance.

United Nations Development Programme, *Public Administration Reform*, Practice Note, (2004) http://www.undp.org/content/dam/aplaws/publication/en/publications/democratic-governance/dg-publications-for-website/public-administration-reform-practice-note-/PARPN_English.pdf.

United Nations Economic and Social Council resolution 2001/45, *Restructuring and revitalization of the Group of Experts on the United Nations Programme in Public Administration and Finance*, http://www.unpan.org/DPADM/CEPA/12thSession/tabid/1544/language/en-US/Default.aspx.

United Nations Economic and Social Council resolution 2006/47 *Report of the Committee of Experts on Public Administration on its fifth session and dates, venue and provisional agenda for the sixth session of the Committee*, preamble.

United Nations, "E-government at the crossroads", *World Public Sector Report*, ST/ESA/PAD/ER.E/49, (2003).

United Nations, *E-Government Survey: E-Government for the Future We Want*, ST/ESA/PAD/SER.E/188, (2014), http://unpan3.un.org/egovkb/Portals/egovkb/Documents/un/2014-Survey/Chapter3.pdf.

United Nations, *E-Government Survey: Leveraging e-government at a time of financial and economic crisis*, ST/ESA/PAD/SER.E/131, (2010).

United Nations, *E-Government Survey: E-Government for the People*, ST/ESA/PAS/SER.E/150, (2012), http://unpan1.un.org/intradoc/groups/public/documents/un/unpan048065.pdf.

United Nations, "Executive summary", *Report of the High-Level Panel of Eminent Persons on the Post-2015 Development Agenda*, (2013), http://report.post2015hlp.org/digital-report-executive-summary.html.

United Nations, "From public administration to governance: the paradigm shift in the link between government And citizens", 2005.

United Nations General Assembly resolution, "International facilities for the promotion of training in public administration", *Official Records of the General Assembly*, Third Session (246 (III) of 4 December 1948).

United Nations General Assembly resolution, *Report of the Ad Hoc Committee on Jurisdictional Immunities of States and Their Property*, A/Res/59/22, (2004), para. 5.

United Nations General Assembly resolution A/68/202, "A life of dignity for all: accelerating progress towards the Millennium Development Goals and advancing the United Nations development agenda beyond 2015", *Report of the Secretary-General from the Sixty-eighth session*, (2013).

United Nations General Assembly, "Lessons learned from the Commission on Sustainable Development," *Report of the Secretary-General*, A/67/757, (2013).

United Nations, "The road to dignity by 2030: ending poverty, transforming all lives and protecting the planet", *Synthesis Report of the Secretary-General on the post-2015 Sustainable Development Agenda*, A/69/700, (2014).

United Nations, "Global economic governance and development", *Report of the Secretary General*, A/67/769, (2013).

United Nations, "Globalization and the state", *World Public Sector Report*, ST/ESA/PAD/SER.26, (2001).

United Nations, *International Developments and Emerging Issues: Recent Trends, Regional and International Developments and Emerging Issues*, (2005), http://unpan1.un.org/intradoc/groups/public/documents/un/unpan020955.pdf.

United Nations, *"Implementation of Agenda 21, the Programme for the Further Implementation of Agenda 21 and the outcomes of the World Summit on Sustainable Development and of the United Nations Conference on Sustainable Development"*, A/68/321, (2013).

United Nations, *My World, The United Nations Global Survey for a Better World*, "We the Peoples Celebrating 7 Million Voices", (2015).

United Nations, *Outcome Document*, Open Working Group for Sustainable Development, Sustainable Development Knowledge Platform: http://sustainabledevelopment.un.org/focussdgs.html.

United Nations, "People matter: civic engagement in public governance," *World Public Sector Report*, ST/ESA/PAD/SER.E/108, (2008).

United Nations, "Promoting empowerment of people in achieving poverty eradication, social integration and full employment and decent work for all", *Report of the Secretary-General*, E/CN.5/2013/3, (2013).

Ibid., Chair's Summary, http://www.un.org/esa/socdev/csocd/2013/summaries/Chairssummaryofdiscussionsonprioritytheme.pdf.

United Nations Public Administration Country Studies, www.UNPAN.org/UNPACS.

United Nations Public Administration Glossary, see definition and explanatory note for "governance", http://www.unpan.org/Directories/UNPublicAdministrationGlossary/tabid/928/language/en-US/Default.aspx.

United Nations Public Administration Glossary, see definition for "government", http://www.unpan.org/Directories/UNPublicAdministrationGlossary/tabid/928/language/en-US/Default.aspx.

United Nations Public Administration Glossary, see definition for "public administration", http://www.unpan.org/Directories/UNPublicAdministrationGlossary/tabid/928/language/en-US/Default.aspx.

United Nations Public Administration Glossary, see definition for "public sector", http://www.unpan.org/Directories/UNPublicAdministrationGlossary/tabid/928/language/en-US/Default.aspx.

United Nations Public Administration Glossary, see definition for "subsidiarity", http://www.unpan.org/Directories/UNPublicAdministrationGlossary/tabid/928/language/en-US/Default.aspx.

United Nations Public Administration Network, www.UNPAN.org.

United Nations, "Realizing the future we want for all", *Report to the Secretary General*, United Nations Task Team on the Post- 2015 Development Agenda, (2012), http://www.un.org/en/development/desa/policy/untaskteam_undf/untt_report.pdf.

United Nations, "Reconstructing public administration after conflict: challenges, practices and lessons learned", *World Public Sector Report*, ST/ESA/PAD/SER.E/135, (2010).

United Nations, *Report of the 5th Session of the Committee of Experts on Public Administration*, E/2006/44–E/C.16/2006/6, (2006).

United Nations, *Report of the 7th Session of the Committee of Experts on Public Administration*, E/2008/44–E/C.16/2008/6, (2008).

United Nations, *Report of the 8th Session of the Committee of Experts on Public Administration*, E/2009/44–E./C.16/2009/5, (2009).

United Nations, *Report of the 12th Session of the Committee of Experts on Public Administration*, E/2013/44–E/C.16/2013/6, (2013).

United Nations, *Report of the High-level Panel of Eminent Persons on the Post-2015 Development Agenda*, (2013).

United Nations, *Report of the Inter-governmental Committee of Experts on Sustainable Development Financing*, A/69/315, (2014).

United Nations, "Resilient people, resilient plant: a future worth choosing." *The Report of the United Nations Secretary-General's High-Level Panel on Global Sustainability, Overview*, (2012), para. 7, http://www.un.org/gsp/sites/default/files/attachments/GSPReportOverview_Letter%20size.pdf.

United Nations, *Rio+20 United Nations Conference on Sustainable Development, Outcome of the Conference: The Future We Want*, A/CONF/216/L.1, (2012), paras., 42, 76 and 101.

United Nations, *United Nations Millennium Declaration*, A/RES/55/2, (2000).

United Nations, "United Nations System Task Team on the Post-2015 UN Development Agenda", *Report to the Secretary-General: Realizing the Future We Want for All*, (2012), para. 49.

United Nations, *The Millennium Development Goals Report 2014*, p. 48.

United Nations, United Nations System Chief Executive Board High Level Committee on Programmes, 26th Session, *Issues Paper by the Vice Chair*, (2013), http://www.unsceb.org/content/action-post-2015-development-agenda-0.

United Nations, "Unlocking the human potential for public sector performance", *World Public Sector Report*, ST/ESA/PAD/SER.E/63, (2005).

United Nations World Commission on Environment and Development, *Our Common Future* (also called Brundtland Report), Oxford University Press (1987), Oxford, U.K.

United Nations, *World Economic Situation and Prospects 2015*, p. 83 (2015), http://www.un.org/en/development/desa/policy/wesp/wesp_archive/2015wesp_full_en.pdf.

Welch, E. W., C. C. Hinnant and M. J. Moon, "Linking citizen satisfaction with e-government and trust in government." *Journal of Public Administration Research and Theory*, (2004), volume 15.

Wit, Joop de, and Akinyinka Akinyoade, "Accountability in formal and informal institutions: a cross country analysis," *Institute of Social Studies*, No. 464, December (2008).

World Bank, *Citizen Voices: Global Conference On Citizen Engagement For Enhanced Development Results*, World Bank Group President Jim Yong Kim, 18 March, (Washington D.C., 2013). ■

www.ingramcontent.com/pod-product-compliance
Lightning Source LLC
Chambersburg PA
CBHW071350280326
41927CB00040B/2753